fashion.

a call

business.

to the light workers

spirituality.

of the fashion industry

FARAH LIZ PALLARO

Publishing Services provided by Paper Raven Books

Printed in the United States of America

First Printing, 2018

Paperback ISBN = 9791220033190
Hardback ISBN = 9791220033206

Table Of Contents

Introduction

It was late 2015, and as usual, I was answering emails from clients even in the midst of the Christmas holiday season. I was feeling a bit down and tired, which, at the time, I thought was because of holiday stress. I would later learn that it was really because of fears that I was holding on to but wasn't aware of back then.

Between clients' emails and some friends' emails, one from a well-known American publishing company stood out. I had never heard of the company, but I was familiar with some of their authors and loved their work. Inside the email was a newsletter offering a package from their auto-publishing branch. When I read it, something really weird happened. I felt a punch in my stomach and heard a very intense, clear voice inside say to me, "You HAVE to write this book."

I was shocked. What book? I am not a writer, and people study years for this. What are you even talking about? Are you crazy, Farah?

But the voice said again, "You have to write this book. Now is the time!"

To this day, how that publishing company got my email address remains a mystery. I never signed up for their newsletter or gave them my information. Yet, somehow, I received it, and I heard that voice so crystal clear that it scared me. Of course, with my typical ego self-sabotage attitude, I decided not to take action back then, and I put it off.

But life had already planned this path for me. And, as the voice said, I had to write this book. After that night, a series of strange and unexpected events led me back to writing a book. I met agents, authors, bookstore owners, book coaches, illustrators, and many other amazing people from the editorial industry whom I had never expected to meet in my wildest dreams! And all of the meetings were chance encounters.

As I am finalizing this book, I still don't know if it will be understood or if the words will resonate. But I decided from the beginning to commit to the process, to leave the outcome to the universe, and to stay true to the inner voice I heard back in 2015.

This book wishes to speak to the fashion industry, but this book is not about fashion. It is not about collections, trends, or seasons. It is about the people in the fashion industry, about their passions, struggles, dreams, decisions, and actions. The message of this book centers around the human aspect of the industry, the awareness of the self, and the spirituality and self-development that comes with self-awareness. Because, as I often say, we create products and services, from people to people, as we dress the world.

I wish to speak with the ones in this industry who are ready to answer the call to join the awakening process, those fashion light workers who are not afraid to take action and make changes the industry desperately needs.

I wish with all my heart that we can create together this journey of healing and improvement by learning to take care of ourselves. In order for true healing to happen, it needs to come from the inside out.

Remember that books come to us when we need them. You are reading this for a reason. So, please, allow that inner voice to speak to you, and trust divine timing. Let's start these changes together. I am here with you.

PART 1

Stepping into the Fashion World: A Student's Journey

Chapter 1

REALIGN YOUR EXPECTATIONS

When I visited a fashion design program for the first time, I fell in love with the atmosphere right away! I felt inspired by the building, constructed completely of white and black materials. The classrooms were full of students' works and crafts—handbags, dresses, sketches, fabrics. As you walked outside, beautiful trees lined the campus, making the students feel set apart and special, yet at the same time buzzing in the center of an exclusive area in metropolitan Madrid.

I made an appointment with the student admissions department and learned more about the courses I could take, the different options for programs of study, and where I could work in my career after graduating. But the conversation with the admissions staff was completely unnecessary. I had already made up my mind and asked her where I should sign. And so, I made my first step into the fashion industry.

When I left the room, I had a huge smile on my face. I was full of energy, feeling happy and inspired. Every time I think back to that moment and how I felt, I compare it with the feeling of being in love. Yes, I was in love. I was in love with my decision. I was in love with a school that I had seen only once and in love with my personal concept of fashion. Yet, neither of these concepts was rooted in reality.

What happened to me is, I'm afraid, a common mistake. All of us in the fashion industry are so driven by the illusion of the fashion system, that we enter school not understanding in detail what we are signing up for. Everything seems perfect, but we are all under the influence of adrenaline and blinded by the promise of being part of an amazing world.

Here is the reality of the fashion industry: there are a lot of bureaucratic systems and calendars, and lots of hard work, all wrapped up (most of the time) in an unhealthy environment. And you experience this immediately in the first week.

When you enter fashion school, you are full of expectations. We all imagine a life full of celebrity parties and exquisite dresses, but the truth is that this will be only 5% of your life in the fashion industry, if you are lucky. What lies beneath the surface-level glamour is hard work, tight calendars, and a very demanding industry.

As with every other career, you will experience struggles and rewards, highs and lows, but in the beginning you have no awareness of this. You think fashion is what you see in the carefully edited shows and the high-profile events. This is all an illusion.

I know the feeling. I was there not so many years ago. But I have survived the fashion industry and have even learned to feel peace, joy, and true fulfillment. I want to tell you what I wish my fashion mentors had told me when I first began.

I am here to be your mentor, sharing with you the secrets of how to live the good life in this crazy fashion world. Breathe, relax, and know that you can find joy in the whole process if you just follow the simple yet powerful advice in this book.

Let's start at the very beginning of your fashion career: surviving and thriving in fashion school.

Chapter 2:

CHOOSING A FASHION SCHOOL

Maybe you are like me, a fool in love with fashion, with the school, with the designs displayed in every classroom. Truth be told, I am still a fool in love with fashion. Love is not simple or easy, but it is a beautiful process, like the growth of a relationship. Your career will not be simple or easy, but it will be beautiful because of the process and your growth as a designer. It's curious how in life most of the time, the answer lies in the process of things. The process is key in fashion school.

The first six months in a fashion school may feel like perfection. I like to call it the Honeymoon Syndrome. For someone who needs beauty around, fashion is a dream come true. I remember those days when I enjoyed everything. I loved being part of the game and most of all having the opportunity to finally call myself a "designer." I now realize how important the title of "designer" was for me at that time. It somehow gave me the sense of being finally in the right category, in the right place, as if by having this label I suddenly fit into society's standards. I was no longer the strange creative girl without a path, but finally a professional with a goal.

It's funny how we allow others to make us believe that we need to have a name or a title to be part of the group. We allow others to deny us the opportunity to simply be ourselves. So, I suppose I was following the American mantra "fake it till you make it," and calling myself designer helped.

But I have to tell you something that scares me. In the last few years that I've been teaching in fashion schools, I see less and less excitement in the entry-level students. Already, during the first month of school, I see frustration, apathy, and loneliness. Why? What happened? Where did the initial excitement go? It used to be that teachers had to motivate students after the first year, to push them not to lose sight of their goal or the excitement and joy that brought them here. But nowadays, I find myself having to do this already in the first month. The new generation of students is a bit cynical. Millennials have been targeted by design companies because millennials will have the money to spend.

The interesting thing about millennials—and maybe this even resonates with you—is that because millennials have typically been raised by two working parents, the schools have played a much larger part in helping them understand the world. They have seen the system behind the product since their earliest years. They are savvy to how the "real world" works, meaning they understand that other people and structures have their own interests at heart. They lose their naivety at an early age, certainly by the time they enter higher levels of education.

If you are a millennial in fashion school, please understand that this tendency toward cynicism is not bad, in and of itself, but you may find that you will need to bolster your own enthusiasm and confidence to survive and thrive fashion school. And we teachers should be here to help you, to guide and mentor you in cultivating your own enthusiasm and confidence, nudging you along from fashion school through the start of your fashion career.

There is a clear problem in today's fashion schools that we need to stop and fix. We need to do something, because it is not okay, and it is our responsibility as professionals in this industry to give to this new generation the right tools to enter the system with an abundance mindset and a perspective of balance, positivity, proactivity, and joy. But, you, reading this book, likely cannot change your teachers or your fashion school. So, what can you do? First, you can make sure you've chosen the right fashion school for *you*.

In my first school, my classmates were sons and daughters of high society members of Madrid: politicians, actors, business owners, *la crème de la crème*. And I felt part of it. I felt like I belonged. The first couple of months, I went to practically every cocktail party. I knew the "right ones" and was fascinated by this magical world that I had always dreamed to be part of. Even though I was not a high society member, I never had struggles with being part of the group during that time. Back then, I was surprised by this, but years later I realized that my gift for empathy made it possible. Empathy has helped me to connect with other people in all the different phases of my life.

At the beginning of my fashion school experience, everything was positive: the people, the courses, the place, the system. I enjoyed it all so much and especially enjoyed being part of the game surrounded by wealthy kids. But one day, obligations began to appear. In order to pay for my studies, I had to work part-time. My father had already paid for my law school, which I dropped out of, and he continued to pay for my home expenses. I felt that he paid enough, and it was up to me to pay for my expensive fashion school tuition. While my heart was in the right place, working part-time started to create rifts between me and the others.

I had less time available compared to my classmates (especially the wealthy ones) and less money to spend on lifestyle and fun. I remember one time we had to go on a trip to Barcelona Fashion Week, and in order to do so, I had to take double shifts at my work to pay for the high costs of the trip. This was the first problem of many problems I would face in my beloved fashion world.

The magic started to fade. I started to understand something crucial: I loved *what* I was doing but not *where* I was doing it. That beautiful, fancy, elegant, and over-the-top school in Madrid had nothing to do with me anymore. So, I started researching new options. I was still very committed the studies, but all that "posh" allure was not fitting my needs anymore. I had to find something more *avant-garde*. I wanted a more "fuck the system!" kind of place.

I was also in my 20s, a truly grunge-indie girl, and, like every member of my generation, was convinced that I could change the world. So, I started with the simplest step: changing my country! The United Kingdom was calling me. London was the obvious choice at that time and had one of the best schools in the field. I wanted to be among the best in the fashion industry, so I knew it was the right choice for me. What I loved about the London fashion school was the energy and the "hands-on" approach. The classrooms were almost like laboratories. We were pushed to create, every day and everything. Instead of buying things, we were supposed to make our own. Clothes, bags, accessories, anything that we would be tempted to go out and buy, we were encouraged to make it ourselves. I loved this approach to bringing creativity fully into my life.

Schools reflect the energy and the cultural dynamics of the city they are in. We often forget how important the environment is, but it is crucial. As a creative thinker, you will be influenced by the energy that surrounds you and this of, course, includes the city. London is an incredible melting pot of ideas. Almost everything is possible there. There are no limits, no boundaries, no judgments. In my experience, it is by far one of the most "free" fashion cities in the world. And the school had the same vibes.

I applied for the Bachelor of Arts program and was accepted. They even accepted credits from my foundation course in Madrid as part of the studies. But I couldn't complete the course load, partly because of time and partly because of money. I couldn't afford to live an entire year in such an expensive city, so I decided to apply for short courses and diplomas. It was a different way of learning to be a designer, but I figured out that piecing together my own coursework fit me perfectly because I am an independent self-starter. Thinking back to that time, I now understand how motivated I was to be part of this industry. I did not allow money and time issues keep me from my studies. I used my creativity to find a solution, and that solution fitted me better than the ordinary way.

I want to tell you something: motivation and intention are powerful tools. Intention and motivation can be your magic if you let them; they will always be there to help you move mountains. If you focus your intent on what you want and allow the energy of motivation to guide you, then miracles will happen. Always.

I had the opportunity to learn to be a designer in a very holistic way. I had a foundation diploma from Madrid with the conventional course structure to learn lots of different things. Then, in London, I had the flexible schedule to choose what to study during the years based on how many courses I could afford. Whether it was fate or a lucky accident, I'm grateful that everything worked out for the best. Today, I realize that this experience helped me so much in my new business adventures, more than I would ever imagine. All of our experiences in life, the good and the bad, are always, *always* for our highest good, even if it is hard to see at first.

In a very eclectic way, I chose to study fabrics and textiles, shoes and bags, illustration, sewing and costume, jewelry, knitting, and research and trends, among many other topics. I wanted to have a 360° vision of fashion. I think this is how fashion studies should be: holistic and eclectic. To be in fashion, you need to learn about lots of things that have *nothing* to do with fashion. Cross-contamination between other forms of fine art, as well as studies, is the key. Fashion needs to be moved forward by acknowledging what is happening in the world. I always tell my students, "Keep one eye on the sewing machine and the other on the news."

When I was a student in London, I was looking for an "avant-garde" approach to fashion, and I found it. I was so happy and felt, once more, that I belonged. But you know what they say, good things never last. The honeymoon feeling soon disappeared. If in the first school I was considered not "cool " enough because I was not a rich girl, in the second school, I was not considered "crazy" or "out of the box" enough. To my teachers and fellow students, I was just another fashion cliché.

Avant-garde was yet another label required of me by others, another blank that I had to fill. It was not enough to be just me, a girl with the passion to create beautiful things that may serve others. Yes, fashion is full of clichés, and so are the fashion schools. The demanding fashion industry had dictated the rules for its soldiers. If you were in the industry in Spain, you were supposed to be classic, rich, and cool. In London, you were expected to be crazy, over the top, and loud. Milan, Paris, and New York all had their own dynamics, as well.

The most curious thing in of all this was the missing of the puzzle: the human factor. I was treated as accepted or not accepted. In both situations, I was excluded for different motivations, but in both cases, I was ultimately excluded. And this had nothing to do with fashion but with something bigger, with what societies dictate, with the concept of being *omologato*, being part of the tribe. And if you don't meet all of the requirements, well, then you are out.

Choosing Your First Fashion School

If you have not yet decided on a fashion school, you are in the perfect place to slow down and make a deliberate decision.

Here are a few things I always recommend my soon-to-be fashion students:

1. Take some summer short courses, just to give you a taste of design. But also be aware that the school's goal may be to sell you on the BA or MA program, so not all the summer schools will necessarily be the right fit. Try to understand first if the program is based on a specific content, like sewing or illustration. If so, this may be useful. However, if the course is too generic, like "Intro to Fashion," then it means that the goal of that short course is to give you a taste of a BA or MA program. Go for the specific course instead.

2. Don't jump straight into a BA program. Look for a school that provides a foundation year. It's an introduction to what you'll study for the next four or five years, and it gives you an awareness. This is a common problem I see in schools, as it is very difficult to find foundation courses in fashion schools. You typically find this type of study in art schools but not always in fashion. My advice here is to search as much as possible, because there are some well-known schools that have them, even if only a few. It's definitely a plus for that school.

3. Look for a teacher who you would want as a mentor. Contact people from the industry and speak with them. You may have to email 20 people to get two phone calls, but that's fine. You're being proactive. If you want to be a fashion designer in a luxury brand, contact designers in a luxury brand. You must try to knock on as many doors

as possible. Don't be shy about this. The best way to gain first-hand information is by speaking with people who are in the role you want to learn about and who are already working in the system.

Use LinkedIn, email someone who is part of an emerging brand, or go to the store or a smaller designer. Or go to fashion week roundtables. Or go to my website. Email *me*! By doing all the above things, you will avoid this fact: 80% of students sign up for a degree the first year and then change before the second year. And this is not happening just in fashion schools but also in universities as well. It is very common, unfortunately.

Making a Change Once You're Already in a Fashion School

If you feel like you've chosen the wrong school, the time to change is now, before you make the same mistake in choosing the wrong fashion brand. Because you want to know what it's really like to work in a shiny brand? The bigger, cooler the name of the brand, the more frustration you will find there. These brands have so much pressure from the system—to sell, communicate, and elaborate codes with high standards—that the demand on employees and collaborators is incredibly high. Fast forward six years to when you're working for that big, flashy brand, and you'll have no idea who you are. You'll be completely burned out.

At this point, realistically, you have two options:

1. Change schools, or even (like I did) change countries! It's never too late to begin again. I know that when

you are in your 20s, it can feel like time is running out. But in the span of your 30-year career, taking an additional year in your school to make sure that you have the right fit could save you years, *decades* of heartache. Back up, reconsider, and choose like you are choosing again for the first time.

2. Make your own path within the school you are attending now. Maybe you are stuck where you are for whatever reason, and that's okay. You can select your classes carefully, seek out that one teacher who "gets" you, find that small group of friends, and create your own smaller environment within the school, tailored to your needs and desires.

You likely feel overwhelmed by your demanding responsibilities and tight schedules, so it's mandatory that you learn to prioritize the important things and declutter all the unnecessary things, so the whole process of building your skills will be more joyful. Don't put too much weight on your shoulders. When you are in your 20s, it's normal to think you can deal with anything. But this is just an illusion. As humans, we all have limits. Once you run up against your limit, acknowledge it and pause; don't push past it.

Don't alienate yourself from the environment, from others, or from the system. You may feel the urge to put on protective armor by developing self-defense mechanisms to protect yourself. We all do this in stressful situations. But in fashion schools, I've seen this many, many times and the result is that you lose touch with the environment. This is so important, my friends. Being fully present in your physical location and connected to the people around you, with all your senses engaged, is the only way you can *feel* rather *think* where your place is.

Develop yourself, your innate talents, as you build your fashion education experience. Don't let yourself be put into one program or one mode of research. Experiment, expand! Find what you love.

Chapter 3:

SURVIVING AND THRIVING IN FASHION SCHOOL

The first thing you need to know is that fashion schools are part of the larger system of the fashion industry. Schools are designed, organized, and structured to teach you what you will find out there in real fashion companies. A fashion school is not a happy island, and the better the school, the more similar to the fashion industry it is.

I have attended three fashion schools and have taught at seven, and all of them are the best in the industry. I've had countless conversations with students who love fashion school, and students who simply do not fit or cannot tolerate the environment. I have seen the patterns come together into some fundamental advice that every single fashion student should hear before day one.

Your school years can become a joyful process if you can let go of those previous expectations and embrace reality, and here is some practical advice that you can use to help you *survive with style.*

Seek out a mentor as soon as you can

Even if you are in your first year, you will need to be looking for a mentor. There's no direct access to how the fashion industry really works, so you need to be close to someone who can tell you the secrets, the reality, and how to achieve success without giving up your life. You will find that teacher's or mentor's words resonate with you, and your intuition will know if they are someone you can trust.

When I was studying at a top fashion school in London, I had an amazing teacher for my course of Bags & Accessories Design. To this day, I remember what she said to me when I was about to show her my designs. I was so nervous and so insecure, questioning myself and doubting that she would like my stuff. As designers, we are always waiting for acceptance and confirmation, but she said to me, "Farah, I am not here to tell you if I like it or not. I am here to help you to understand if it is properly made or not. I may not buy your bags, but for sure someone will." In that moment, I understood the difference between teaching and mentoring. She was more than a teacher. She was mentoring me toward becoming a confident, skilled designer.

Talk to people with experience, people you find empathy with, people you trust. When I was in school, I didn't have a direct mentor. I modeled my teachers and learned many things the hard way, but I wish I'd known to intentionally seek out a mentor from the beginning.

Adjust your attitude

When you approach a project, even if it's for a class, don't complain about the deadlines. Don't focus on just the superficial. This is your opportunity to approach a deadline like a professional—centered, decisive, proactive.

In everything in life, but especially in the fashion industry, 20% of your success is skill and 80% is attitude and approach. The attitude and the approach you have, not only in fashion school but also in life, will make the difference. In companies, there will be always someone more prepared than you, equally prepared as you, and, yes, worse than you. How will your boss and your team choose who they prefer to work with? Always, attitude makes the difference.

In every class I teach, I find at least one or two students with a bad attitude. This number seems to increase every year, which I think reflects the increase in frustration levels in fashion schools. While society is demanding awareness, mindfulness, and a better approach to life, we are still stuck in our fashion bubble, and we simply avoid zooming out and seeing the context where we are.

When I see students with a bad attitude, I understand what lies behind it—a looming sense of insecurity, a lack of belonging, and frustration. Their bad attitude is just a coping mechanism to create armor to protect themselves from the feelings they so desperately do not want to acknowledge. When you develop a bad attitude, you hate everything around you, but you simply can't get away from the same feelings, people, situations. You are attracted to what you most want to push away, like a moth to a flame, and sooner or later you will burn out.

A good attitude starts with the awareness that everything happens in your life for a reason. Everything. You may not be aware of what the reason is in the moment, but as years pass by, you will see how everything aligns. As Steve Jobs said, "You can't connect the dots looking forward; you can only connect them looking backwards."

A good attitude involves always seeing the bright side of things, I know it may sound naive, but I always say that there are two ways you can live this life: by seeing all the negative or seeing all the positive. I choose the last one, because I choose to live a happy life. In any case, things will happen, and I may not have control over all of them, but at least I have control over how I react to them.

Let me ask you this question: how do you wish to live, happy or bitter? "Happiness is an inside job" is a quote that pops on Pinterest all the time and for good reason!

Focus on learning the craft, not just designing something beautiful

The more you learn about the fashion industry, the more you realize that it is full of concrete production processes, and this is part of the beauty of it. What lies behind the product, the services, and the creative process is hours spent in craft and innovation. When you will learn the craft, then all will make sense, and you will understand how the magic happens: craft plus creativity.

Focus on learning all the technical aspects of product, all the ingredients that create the perfect meal. You do not have to be the one who creates the raw material if this scares you, but just like a chef, you need to know as much as possible about the ingredients in order to cook the perfect meal. You do not need to tan leather yourself, but you should take any opportunity to learn from a specialist who does tan leather.

I live in Italy, where the most important years of my career were built, first in Milan and then in Florence. I had the opportunity to learn what "made in Italy" truly looks like, smells like, feels like, and tastes like. When people ask me what Italy is all about, I always use the example of coffee. Why is Italian coffee so good? It's not because of the coffee beans, but because of the high-quality machines and those amazing baristas who know that a proper cappuccino is ⅓ espresso, ⅓ steamed milk, and ⅓ velvety foam. This, my friend, is how the perfect cappuccino is created, and it is the whole process, from bean to mug at my favorite cafe.

To become a master of the craft, you have to add love to all you create.

Be proactive

This is probably one of the most important pieces of advice in this book. You have to show passion for what you do and approach the whole process from an abundance mindset.

Millennials, you have easy access to the Internet. And this is a fact, especially when you compare your student years to the student years of people who are now senior designers, twenty years older than you. Having the Internet is good, because you have so much information and inspiration, but at the same time (please hear me out on this), I worry that it's making you lazy. Plus, the Internet lies!

When I teach about the research process before starting a project, I always encourage my students to use both desk research (computer, books, and Internet) and field research (going out into the world). This industry wants proactive people. Period. Fashion companies are looking for people who don't wait for direction all the time, but people who are always ready with new ideas, alternatives, and energy.

And you have to be proactive from *day one* in the school. Don't expect your teacher to give you the foolproof syllabus and rubric. Don't expect that every assignment will give you everything you need to know and how to do it, and how you'll be graded, all right away. In the real world, you won't receive briefs. You'll have to figure it out. So, start now.

Lots of people want to work in this industry, but if you aren't proactive, you won't make it in the fashion industry. Being proactive is something that goes hand-in-hand with having the right attitude. Proactivity comes when you add intention to an action. It is not just acting, not just making a movement for the sake of moving. It is acting with a purpose.

And can I tell you the secret behind people who are proactive and how they continue to be motivated and inspired to chase their design concepts? There are two types of people in the world: the ones who choose to see abundance and the ones who choose to see lack.

The main emotions that move us are love and fear. With that in mind, I offer you a challenge. Set this book down for just a few seconds, and look at the people around you. Look at how she is walking across the street, how he is talking to the person sitting next to him, or how she is holding the expression on her face. Is the person you're watching acting from love or fear?

Day-to-day, moment-to-moment, are *you* acting from love or fear? People who are proactive operate from love. They *love* the craft of fashion, and they desire to learn, develop, and grow in their own talent. What's more is that proactive people believe there is plenty of inspiration everywhere in the world, in every moment. They believe in an *abundance* of inspiration. This is why proactive people are always chasing. They believe there's something just in front of them. And they are often right.

Proactivity comes from passion, and passion comes from joy and fulfillment. Use these powerful emotions from day one at school. It will pay you back tenfold throughout your career as a fashion designer. Trust me.

Begin to see the spiritual side

All of these practical things are important and are things I would tell to any fashion student to help that person truly grow while in fashion school. But, there are some deeper truths behind these practical pieces of advice, and these deeper truths are exactly what separate the successful, joyful, fulfilled designers from the hollow, empty, burned-out designers.

I am giving you advice about the outside world that you can use in a simple way every day, but I also want to show you that there is a bigger answer that encompasses everything. In every situation you will face, all reactions will come from either fear or love.

As you take action in following this advice, you'll find yourself growing and becoming more aware of yourself, your inner life. And your inner life is precisely the point of this book because, as self-development expert Wayne Dyer says, the answer is inwards. This is where spirituality intersects with the fashion world. As I grow older and gain more experience, I realize that there is a spiritual answer for everything, a bigger box that encompasses the whole.

We've just talked about four very practical things you should know while you are a student in fashion school:

1. Seek out a mentor.

2. Adjust your attitude.

3. Focus on learning the craft, not designing just something beautiful.

4. Be proactive.

But if you simply apply these pieces of advice, you will still be missing something—the inner part of your soul that desires to be, yes, a great designer, but also a bold, powerful inspiration whose life is full and joyful and passionate. You get to this place of holding both, the skill of being a top designer and the joy of a fulfilling life, and by always looking for the spiritual truths underneath the practical.

Let me show you the spiritual underpinnings of these four practical lessons. We talked about mentoring. A mentor is also a spiritual guide, a source who will guide you in your action and your growth. Practically, yes, you need a mentor to help you make connections in the industry, but spiritually, you need someone who will help you expand your wisdom as you grow in your career. When you read holy books of any religion, they all speak about mentoring and guidance. It is crucial to have a "go-to person," both practically as well as spiritually.

We talked about your attitude, but I know that when students have bitchy attitudes, at the heart, they are actually afraid. They fear judgment and not being good enough. They are protecting themselves from rejection. If they could take actions out of love, rather than fear, then they would have an attitude that would help them succeed in the fashion industry.

Learning the craft has also a spiritual meaning. When you learn a craft, you must experience it, and in fashion this involves action and using your senses. To draw, to sew, to cut, to build, you are putting focus on the body, not just on the mind. When you sew, there is a connection between mind, body, and soul as you create, bringing everything together as one whole. Do you know why doing yoga is so good for mindfulness? It follows the same principle: you connect mind and body and live in the present moment of the action. This is why it's so important to learn the craft, not just to gain technical skill, but also because it will drive you to the physical action that will embrace: Mind + Body + Being Present.

To be proactive is to have an abundance mindset. Proactivity involves action and intention. First, it takes you away from the passive state. Then, it pushes you to move forward, toward growth. To be proactive means to believe that you will achieve your goal because you see opportunity. Seeing opportunity is seeing the bottle full rather than empty. This, my friends, means to have a mindset of abundance rather than lack.

Throughout this book, I will be sharing with you both the concrete strategies that you will need to survive day-to-day, but also the intangible ways to uncover your inner self, which will guide you to become the centered, passionate designer you know you are.

Chapter 4

BEGIN TO LOVE YOURSELF

I once had a classmate named Anna who had the most gifted hands I have ever seen. She could draw beautifully, as if there was a perfect connection between her hand and her brain. Even with her talent, she couldn't handle school. She was very sensitive, and even a little feedback on her art would cause her to burst into tears. She leaned into her talent of drawing, but she couldn't concentrate on getting better in the craft, because *she didn't love herself.* If she received one hint of disapproval from a teacher or fellow student, she heaped *loads* of disapproval onto herself and simply shut down.

And let me tell you what happens when you do not love yourself: you attract more of that. You attract people who will always remind you that you do not love yourself by treating you badly, because deep down inside, you believe you deserve to be treated that way. We attract what we are.

Gifted as she was, Anna left the fashion industry because she could not love herself. I never heard from her again. I hope she has a beautiful and fulfilled life, whatever path she has chosen. I truly believe we all find our path in life, sooner or later, but it is a shame that she left school, because her art could have contributed great beauty to modern fashion.

You may not be aware of your value or talents, and this, my friend, is so common in our society, not just in fashion. It is heartbreaking that we do not take time to get to know ourselves better. Instead, we spend so much energy focusing on what others do and trying desperately to understand how others might react.

I learned about the concept of self-love years ago. Honestly, it sounded stupid to me at first. What do you mean by "loving yourself?" I do love myself, of course! That is the first lie we all tell ourselves. If it is true that you really love yourself, then you will take time to get to know yourself better, to nurture yourself, and to gain clarity and awareness of yourself. This is the only way to understand your strengths.

You may want to receive validation at school, from your peers, colleagues, and teachers, and that is okay—it is human—but you have to believe in yourself, too. Have a clear understanding of this: *when God was creating you, God gave you your own ability to create.* Imagine that you are in a long row of beautiful humans full of light, ready to go to this three-dimensional world to create with purpose, and when God stands in front of you, He says, "No, you there, you'll go without creativity." Absurd, right? We *all* have creative skills, as we all have analytical skills. Now, some have developed their creative skills, and some are only just beginning, but we can all grow in creativity.

I often ask students in my class to do this simple yet powerful exercise to discover their individual talents, and I encourage you to do so now, too.

Write three lists, each of five items:

1. Five things you love to do.

2. Five things that you know you're good at, that your family and friends ask for your help with.

3. Five things that you just love about life, even simple things like a beautiful cappuccino.

Look back over your three lists. Hold the image of doing, seeing, touching, tasting each of these things. When you hold one in your mind, do you feel something move inside of you? Imagine you're in love and feel those butterflies. When you think of what you love to do, you feel those butterflies. That's the hint that this is your talent.

Maybe you haven't developed your talent yet. Maybe you're not as good as someone else at this thing. But maybe this is your hint that your soul wants to explore this more. When you love yourself, you will allow yourself to explore this thing more, whatever it is—drawing, sewing, fabrics, coffee, whatever sets those butterflies alight in your soul.

Loving yourself and having awareness of who you are will be your GPS in this fashion world.

Trust this. It will always lead you to a beautiful place, and I've seen this many times with all the students who had the courage to go back to what is important, to learn about the true meaning of life, to take care for themselves first as an individual, and ultimately take it with them to their fashion careers.

Martha was a student of mine seven years ago. She went on to start her own brand and on the outside was achieving enviable success. But she felt something was missing in her life. She moved back to her small hometown in the countryside of East Serbia. She's very close to her grandmother and her friends, bonded by the survival of war as is the case in many countries in Europe. These amazing women are producing needlework with techniques that have been all but lost, but with Martha's help, they're now sending this needlework to big brands in Berlin. She combined her own self-love and proactive nature to create a beautiful business, a business from the heart that makes her happy. Now, she lives a fulfilled life.

Do not obsess about going to work for the fancy, new, cool company that is the "hot brand" of the moment just to name drop. First, question who you are and what things makes you happy in life. These are your priorities: the city you live, the lifestyle you want to achieve, love, relationships, healthy environments. It's not just about work and fashion. Do not give your all to one single component. You can have all of them if you take the time to be fully one with yourself and say out loud what you really want and what makes you happy. Finally, don't compare yourself too much. You lose value when you compare yourself to others. Instead, give yourself value.

Learn to love yourself now, and success will follow you, in school and in your career as a designer.

Chapter 5:

SPIRITUAL TIPS FOR THE STUDENT'S LIFE

Many young designers feel that they could succeed in the fashion industry if it weren't for some external factor: a bitchy teacher or boss, inhumane deadlines, judgmental colleagues. The industry will always be filled with problems like these. If you want to survive and *thrive*, know that you will not be able to change the entire industry, but you *can* change how you react to these problems. And this begins with developing yourself first. As you develop yourself, your everyday actions will be helping improve this industry.

Every interaction in the fashion industry is an interaction with a *person*. I say this all the time to my students, as well as my clients, "Companies are made by people, not robots… yet!" In the courses I teach, I ask my students to do the following exercise in class. I ask them to make a list of the

10 things they struggle the most with the fashion industry. It always amazes me that 80% of the things they struggle with are personal issues, not technical or methodological.

Below is a list of some of the most common things students point out, year after year:

1. Dealing with people with big egos and bad attitudes.

2. Superficiality and the lack of respect.

3. The lack of humanity in working environments.

4. Demanding requests and fast pace.

5. How the industry treats women.

6. Labeling people.

7. Lack of identity.

8. Focusing too much on the aesthetics and not enough on the content.

9. Being constantly judged.

10. Too many hours of work and not enough pay.

Do you see the common pattern? It is all related to the human factor, the self, the person, the dynamics between people. Not practical things, like that the drawings have to always be done with pantone pencils rather than markers, or that the sewing machines don't work properly in ateliers, or that in marketing departments you have to use PowerPoint rather than Indesign. No, they do not point out these things.

Rather, they all point to problems that are simply aspects of being human, to personal issues that affect all of us.

So, we need to get to the core of things as soon as possible, to what really matters, and try to solve it. Otherwise, we will continue to add to the problem that has existed for years and years.

Do you want to succeed in fashion school and, ultimately, the fashion industry? Let's dive deep into *your* human factor.

"We are not human beings having a spiritual experience. We are spiritual beings having a human experience," was originally expressed by philosopher Pierre Teilhard de Chardin but has since been repeated by nearly all of the most influential spiritual and self-development authors. It took me a while to understand this simple principle. We are more than we see, yet what we see determines what we do; therefore, what we think is what we are.

I understand it may sound like some sort of New Age-hilly-yuyu-alien-strange thing, but the understanding of the inner self is key. The better relationship you create with your inner self, the better life you will have. Once I understood this concept, which inside of all of us resides something holy and pure that connects us with a bigger and greater source, the less lonely, helpless, and afraid I felt.

You believe in you, and others will believe in you. If you learn to love yourself, others will and so on. All of this starts from the very simple action of connecting with yourself. I know what you are saying: "Okay, all this sounds great, but how I do this? "We are very lucky to live in an era where information is so accessible. They call it the awakening and human knowledge era. We have access to techniques that have helped people for centuries to become more centered, peaceful, and joyful.

Nowadays, it is so easy to learn do meditation, yoga, meridian tapping, visualizations, affirmation, mindfulness, and so on. If you don't know these concepts yet, don't worry. I will introduce you to them shortly. These are just some of the many techniques out there to help you turn down the volume of outside noise, so you can properly hear yourself. And after you hear yourself, you just have to pay attention to what that inner voice tells you. That voice you will hear is exactly the voice you have to pay attention to—your inner GPS, your Google maps, your driver.

We all know inside what is best for us. The answer is always inward, like Wayne Dyer said, but we obsess with the absurd search for answers outside of ourselves. We somehow believe that others will give us the meaning of our lives and the directions we need to take, when really everything we need to know is already inside ourselves from day one. We often follow what others suggest but forget that the final choice needs to be ours. Every decision we make is crucial for our future.

I encourage you to own who you are. Have the courage and invest the time to understand who you are. Even as you're doing homework for a class, you are also reading for your own development. They are both critical for your success in this world. The essence of you will infuse every project, every collection you design, and every idea you developed in all of that material. In every creation, in every piece, will always be *you*.

A collection should be a group of ideas connected by a central concept. Yet, from my students, I often see projects in which the ideas are amazing but not connected, and therefore there is no concept. Over years of observation, I have realized that students present projects that, though beautiful, are not connected with a central concept because they do not have an awareness of who they are. The project is developed from a place of uncertainty. As a result, there is no clarity in the project because there is no clarity in the self.

If you focus on developing yourself first by understanding your whole self—your fears and loves, the good and the bad—and then embracing all of them without judgement by focusing on them and acknowledging that they are part you, then you will be in perfect and direct connection with your own source, your inner self, the main source of creation. And this is exactly when magic happens. Everything suddenly makes sense. Finally, you find peace of mind and enjoy the process.

I truly believe that self-development and spirituality should be taught in fashion schools. Just as there is History of Fashion, there should be History of Spirituality, because some of the most amazingly creative work designers have accomplished involved spirituality. Since those courses do not exist, I am writing this book for you. Someday, I plan to build my own fashion school where fashion and spirituality, creative management and self-development, are all taught. If T. Harv Eker can combine money and spirituality in business, why can't we do the same with fashion and spirituality? Spirituality is the basis of it all.

When I teach that first course, History of Spirituality, this very chapter will be the foundation of the content. In fact, I will give you your syllabus for personal development when you are in school, especially in your early years. All of these authors are gifts. Their words will resonate somehow in you. You cannot feel lonely or lost if you read some of these amazing people.

> *Your Erroneous Zones* by Wayne Dyer
> *Creative Visualization* by Shakti Gawain
> *The Power is Within You* by Louise Hays
> *Ask and It Is Given* by Esther and Jerry Hicks
> *The Power of Now* by Eckhart Tolle
> *Live in the Moment* by Eckhart Tolle

In addition to your reading list, I have a list of habits to practice for self-development, in much the same way as you practice habits as a designer. I am not a guru or spiritual guide, but I personally try to implement all of these habits in my everyday life. I am just someone who tries to evolve, progress, and become better each day. These have all made a positive difference in my life, and I want you to test them out for yourself and see the results in your own life.

Learn to breathe

Yes, I know what you are thinking: "Come on, Farah! I know how to breathe!" My question to you is, "Are you *sure*?" Did you know that we often experience apnea by breathing with short breaths? If you do not breathe properly, there is not enough oxygen in your body and brain. Yogis have said that the breath is the connection with God. Why? Because if you do not breathe, you die. Simple as this. God is life, and life is God.

When I feel stressed, I stop whatever I am doing and breathe deeply for two *full* minutes. Just this single gesture rebalances. Every time you start to feel any kind of negative emotion—stress, anxiety, fear, anger, doubt—breathe deeply. Allow the oxygen to fill you up and all will be instantly better.

Practice gratitude every day

When you wake up and you are in that beautiful moment, just as your eyes are opening and seeing the light of the room, take a second to think of at least three things you are grateful for. List them and then say, "Thank you God/Universe/nature," whatever you believe in. Do the same when you go to sleep.

Gratitude is a powerful tool, because it puts you in an abundance mindset rather than a lack mindset. You focus on what you have, not what you lack. As soon as I wake up, I give gratitude for at least three things in my life. After this, I offer a little prayer to the angels asking them to take care of me during the day and guide me through the challenges I may have to face. By doing this, the universe will give you more, because you are sending the message of "Hey, I like what I have, and I would love to have more of it!"

Spiritual guides and self-development teachers over the centuries have advised that what you focus on expands. Be intentional about putting your focus on what you're grateful for, and watch the goodness in your life expand before your very eyes.

Practice daily movement

This doesn't just mean go to the gym (although if gyms are your thing, that's great). Rather, it means, find ways to move throughout the day. You can choose to walk instead of taking the bus, take the stairs instead of the elevator, run for 10 minutes, or practice yoga for 15 minutes. You can do whatever you prefer.

When you make your body work and move, you feel alive. You are in the now as you are focusing on your body and not fixating on the mind, lost in the thoughts. Now, you can truly *hear* yourself, your intuition.

Reward yourself

Every day, choose one simple action to give love to yourself. It could be something simple as a 15-minute nap, a healthy meal, a manicure, a massage, or a book for fun. Rewarding yourself for all the effort you make every day is important. By doing this, you are putting yourself in a place of priority and telling yourself that you deserve all those things, that you deserve better.

You do not have to spend money to do so. Your reward could be anything that is precious to you. For example, my everyday reward is five minutes of meditation and walks with my dog. Those things are priceless to me. Every day, regardless of what happens, I try to reward myself by making time and space to do these lovely things.

Protect your energy

Our energy is so important that it's mandatory you learn to protect yourself. We often give too much during our day—at work, at school, with others—that we forget how all these actions and people around us are draining our energy. Our bodies need eight hours of sleep for a good reason: we need to re-establish our energy level to be able to deal with the day ahead.

I've learned that if I do not protect myself and maintain awareness of the energy I'm using and the situations and people that are draining, I get to the point where both my mind and body become weak, and I'm more likely to suffer from anxiety, depression, and health issues.

Protecting your energy starts with the awareness that you have to rest. Give value to the energy you give to others, and make sure that by doing so you are not drawing too much from yourself.

Your energy, your inner light, is precious. If you do not protect it and make sure you keep some for you, you're more vulnerable to all sorts of issues, including personal and health problems.

Life is about giving and taking equally, and it is important that you learn to receive and keep energy as much as you give in order to find balance. Always keep this present with you: protect your energy, keep some light for you, and take care of yourself.

RECAP: Your Student Designer Spiritual Toolkit

These tips may seem simple in concept, but they are powerful in practice. Keep them in your toolkit, and use them every day. Every. Single. Day.

1. Pause to breathe

2. Practice gratitude

3. Find movement

4. Reward yourself

5. Protect your energy

You will be the shining light for your friends, your classroom, and soon your own pocket of the fashion industry. We need *your* light; protect it.

Chapter 6

TRAIN YOUR DESIGN EYE

As you are cultivating your inner world, you will also be changing how you see your outer world. To develop yourself as a designer is simple: be curious, always. Understand the environment in which you are working. Zoom out, and understand what is surrounding you—the structure, the people, the system, everything. Study the dynamics. The people and brands in the fashion world are going to be completely new to you, nothing like you've ever experienced in high school or the working world. Fashion schools create beautiful environments with crafts, art, and architecture. The school's goal is to keep you inspired. And to be inspired means to be "In-Spirit" as Wayne Dyer used to say.

Use all your senses. As soon as you start being comfortable with using all your senses, you will develop your intuition. Your intuition will be your secret weapon in this industry, because you will soon be paid for how you see the world that surrounds you, filtered through your lens and the beauty you see in things. The way you create is the way you see things. It's as simple as that.

It's necessary that you analyze your physical surroundings in order to have a better understanding of what your eye reacts to and what you are naturally interested in. Then, you can apply that vision to a collection, an illustration, or a project, anything. Whatever it is, you need to own it! Own that you are a fashion student, a designer, a creative thinker. Own what you have inside, your creativity, and what you have to share with the world. Make a list of things that catch your eye everywhere you go. Develop the habit of carrying a notebook or some way to write down all ideas, a place to free your mind and explore: Inspiration + Investigation + Process = Creation.

Being a designer or a creative thinker means being naturally curious about everything. Ask yourself, "Why?" as much as possible. This question is the most useful way to move your creative juices! Be curious about art, architecture, history, current events, knowledge from all areas. We call this "cross-contamination." Prada finds inspiration in contemporary art and opened a gallery with her own personal collection. Armani takes his designs from architecture and joined a team of architects early on in his career. These are truly curious people, and they bring inspiration from outside the design industry to create something new. This is completely different than taking an idea that another designer has and replicating it.

Curiosity will always lead to innovation. So, take all that curiosity, apply it, and make it concrete! Try different outputs to help you do this: writing, drawing, sewing, watercolors, anything that sounds fun or interesting. This way you will slowly understand the tools for creation that suit you best, and by acknowledging this you will understand the type of designer you are.

Think also about the type of professional and personal relationships you're building. The way we think, and our daily actions, are conditioned by the people who surround us. If you are surrounded by people who always tell you that achieving your dreams is not realistic, then it will become impossible to you. But, if you surround yourself with positive people who think anything is possible in this world, then you will achieve literally anything you want in life.

This applies to fashion schools, too. Surround yourself with mavericks, and you will always think outside of the box. Surround yourself with people who are curious about culture, and you will become a cultural person as well. As humans, we model people by copying others' actions and behaviors. Make sure the ones you choose in the fashion school reflect what you want to become and achieve. The same holds true for teachers. It's more important to choose your classes based on who is teaching the class than what the class is about. Teachers have the power to model enthusiasm for a topic, and that enthusiasm will spark your curiosity.

Of course, you will have to learn content, like making patterns or business models or retail management, but you can learn these topics in many ways. Fashion school is a unique opportunity to learn from professionals with whom you might otherwise never have such a close relationship. There will be opportunities to attend workshops or guest lectures from an important person, maybe the art director of a luxury brand. Your fellow students may talk about networking and making backstage connections. Particularly in the third year, students want to meet and greet with highly visible people in the industry. But, honestly, those big brand art directors do not even want to talk to you about working for them until you've learned all the skills you need to do the job. Complete your work, do it well, and then networking will follow.

Movers and shakers in fashion will want to see that you are a confident designer with skills, curiosity, and a willingness to take risks. When I was a student, I always surrounded myself with people who were not afraid to take risks, people who wanted to make the change and become leaders. Years later, many of them became just that, leaders in this fashion industry. I wanted to lead, so I knew that I had to surround myself with people who got me, who supported my ideas. And I supported them, too.

If, in my first years as a fashion student, I had chosen to be with the ones who were following the status quo, I wouldn't have had the courage to move from Madrid to London and then back to Madrid. I wouldn't have had the courage to start my own business and, more recently, to write this book! My actions, in some way, were conditioned and supported by all those amazing creative thinkers who surround me back then, the people I chose as close colleagues and friends. And all of them were there for a reason. Meeting people at school is not random; you meet them for a reason, and you may not understand it now, but you will someday, even if it will take you 15 years or more!

Let me tell you about Shannon, a classmate in London. We were together in a bag making course over the summer.

Almost all students in that course were English, except for Shannon, myself, and another Spanish friend we'd met in that course. Shannon was so talented that I admired her from the first day of class. She was, and is, an amazing designer. Not only that, but she is also a great storyteller, full of creativity. It is crazy how her brain can develop ideas almost effortlessly. I always felt as if she was the teacher and I was the student.

We were all afraid of showing our ideas, but she was a volcano of ideas and confident that her proposals were going to be successful. She owned her brilliance. Even though she was humble and helpful and simple, she still stood apart from the rest. She was connected to a creative source. I felt back in those days that she was the most creative of all of us at school. After school, we lost touch with each other. She went back to India, and I went back to Madrid. Years passed, but I've continued talking about her every time I reminisce with someone about my school years in London. Whenever I have to describe an amazing designer, I describe Shannon.

Now, after nearly 15 years in the fashion industry, I am a consultant and a teacher in a very important fashion school in Florence. This year we had a new master's degree course in creative art direction. I was teaching a class on collection management, and on the first day, I saw a familiar face sitting at the table. Shannon was one of the students in my course. When we first saw each other, we hugged and laughed so loudly! I couldn't believe that we would meet again in such a strange way so many years later. This time, our roles reversed. She was the student, and I was the teacher.

She came to this master's program after almost 20 years of owning a brand, because she was close to burning out. Her brand had success but took almost all of her energy away. Now I know why life put her on my path again—so I could mentor her and help her see that she is more than a brand, more than a label, that she is a beautiful human being with an amazing talent called creativity.

I share this story with you to show you that the way I figured out how to develop as a designer was by focusing on developing *methodology*. As a fashion student, you will be taught many specific skills, crafts, and content but will not necessarily be taught the methodology that will enable you to fully progress as a designer. You need to figure out the methodology that best fits you. When I teach this to my students, I ask them to focus on just a few steps.

Be obsessively curious

About everything! Ask yourself, "Why?" as much as possible. Why do these colors go so well together? Why do these shapes catch my eye? Why did the designer focus on that concept? Curiosity always leads to imagination, always! And imagination is crucial to being a top designer.

Feed your creativity

This is linked to curiosity, of course. Designers are always up-to-date with the latest trends, art exhibitions, movies, events, and so on. They attend all of these to feed and stimulate their creativity. You need to learn the habit of feeding your beautiful, magical brain with creative information in order to build ideas.

Experiment

We learn from our mistakes, not our successes. Well, this also applies to becoming a good designer. You need to experiment to understand what type of craft you prefer, what type of designs you love, and what type of creative environment stimulates you. Experiment through your sketchbook, with your sewing machine, or by painting. Whatever your heart tells you to try, try it. And know that mistakes are the best way to learn.

Books, books, and more books

Become a book lover, a reader fetishist, a nerd of culture. Whatever you wish to call it, make a habit of reading a book every single week, if not more! Read novels, history books, art books, or whatever type of source that you feel attracted to. Throughout my career, the best ideas I ever developed were inspired by books I read. I was inspired by Agatha Christie's mysteries, Frida Kahlo's biography, the costume details described in Isabel Allende novels, and of course the history of Cristobal Balenciaga. A book opens a magical portal. It connects you straight away with the source of creativity.

And I always say, the book you choose to read ends up in your hands for a reason. It's no coincidence. Even this book you've found and are reading for a reason.

There are many other methodologies and habits that you can apply. You need to find yours and make use of them to become the designer you dream to be. The list above is a good starting point. Still, I must advise you that developing yourself as a designer is only half of the journey toward living the good life as a designer. Shannon had certainly developed herself as a designer, but she experienced that burnout and lost all of her energy because she had not also developed her own inner world. Developing your skills, curiosity, and creativity goes hand-in-hand with developing yourself as a deep, centered person.

In my own classes in the master's program, I teach these very practices. Even though the course is focused on technical methodology for fashion management, we also cover the simple wisdom of self-development, which is what I share with you here in this book.

Chapter 7

RESEARCH

Fashion schools are organizations that teach you professional methodology to survive and build a professional fashion career. They teach you how to draw, sew, and build projects. But they do not educate you on how to create. If you are lucky, you will find teachers who understand the importance of teaching you to develop your talents, your inner you first, so that afterward you can develop the necessary skills you will need as a top designer. It is important to build your thoughts and emotions before you put them on paper to draw a collection or build a project.

You must learn how to create on command. In the fashion industry, we have tight calendars and very demanding expectations. Tasks and deadlines come so fast that often you have no time to enjoy the creative process. The secret to creating on command is building an awareness of who you are and your unique creativity before you start to run.

When you are creating, you feel connected. With your creative process and with everything that surrounds you, there is almost a mystical force that moves you. This is the beauty of creation. It moves emotions inside your heart, coursing through your body. You've experienced some of this already. It's what has brought you to fashion school.

When I ask students, "What is research?" they say...
    "A report,"
    "Learning about a subject,"
    "Creating mood boards,"
    "Filling up a sketchbook."

But they are telling me about the *result*. They've missed the research *process*. Often, all the things they describe as research are the result of research, not the research itself.

To research is human

Research is something all humans do. It comes from the stimulus of observation. At its core, research is observation and awareness. Every single day and in every situation, we are doing research. We may not be aware of it, but our subconscious mind is always observing and analyzing.

Research is psychology. We are influenced by external factors and internal factors. External factors could be society, politics, music, art, or architecture. Internal factors might include your family's culture, your personal values, or your own memories and history. We draw on all of these things when we research. There is no limit to where your research can come from.

So, again, we go back to being curious and to the fact that you need to be a sponge, absorbing everything around you.

During my years as a student, and later on as a teacher, I always forced myself and my students to add research to the process of building ideas for their projects. I had them spend as much time as possible doing field research and desk research, so as to fill their head with infinite possibilities and as much visual and verbal information as possible.

Without research, innovation cannot exist. And in fashion, we know we need to innovate ourselves after each season ends. Every six months, we need to revisit the external factors around us and the internal factors that reside within us in order to create something completely new.

With some companies, you can see their external and internal influences by looking at their campaigns. For example, there is a luxury Italian brand that shows their designs in the context of a big, Italian family having a meal together. In that scene, you can see how research has been influenced by their external factors (Italian culture of sharing meals with large families) and internal factors (personal history and values related to family).

Discover your own research methodology

What I mean by this is that, yes, you will build a methodology for sure, but before that, you need to know your creative side and how it operates.

Once you start working, you will have to create for others. And quickly. Or create for yourself in a very small amount of time. The pressure will be a heavy weight on your shoulders. Learning what touching points move you into the creative process will train you for the real world in companies.

Picture yourself as a five-year-old child every time you are doing research. Observe things as if you are seeing them for the first time, and question everything in every shape and form. What colors do you like? What forms catch your eye? What atmospheres inspire you the most? What type of other forms of art? I spent my school years learning about my natural colors, the ones that my eye saw in everything no matter what, what materials I felt inspired by, what other sources of art pushed my creativity. I was obsessively curious about everything.

Try this out for yourself. Allow your eye to react to the colors, shapes, materials, situations, the world that surrounds you. Don't force it. Put your mind in a curious mode, and just ask your eye to find something interesting. Naturally, you will notice one color and not another, or will observe how one person is dressed and not another one. Don't judge why one is catching your eye and not the other. Let yourself react. I might notice a woman with short, curly, dark hair, and I remember my grandmother. There's no judgment; it's simply a noticing. The moment your eye reacts to something, write it down. After a few years, you will find a pattern in what your eye catches, whether it's a similar color scheme or pattern. It will be uniquely yours.

Make a habit of researching once a week, not just immediately before a project. Research will be critical for your career and development as a designer. Set aside the time to simply let your eye wander and take notes. It's play! But only if you can *relax* into the play. When you can play and research at the same time, you will emerge as a phenomenal designer.

Keep your head and your heart light

Michael Wolff, designer and colorist, always says, "If you walk through life with your head full of pre-occupations, you will not notice anything." Have you ever been to a big city, full of incredible colors, buildings, performers, and food, and the people there are walking around completely preoccupied with something else? They don't even seem to see the world happening around them. We all do this, for sure, but as a designer, it's literally our job to pause, push aside the pre-occupations, and be fully aware of the world around us.

Curiosity and free-thinking are key when you are in the research process. When you are nervous, anxious, or stressed, be sure to re-center yourself before you research. Go back to those tips I shared in Chapter 5. Breathe, practice gratitude, find movement, reward yourself, and protect your energy. These things will shift your mind from preoccupied to play.

Remember, being able to research continuously will make you worth paying when you become a designer, and doing research will help you stay a happy, fulfilled designer and love your life.

Chapter 8

GO TO WORK

Work as soon as possible. That being said, do not quit your studies for a job. At least once every year one student comes to me asking me, "Prof, should I finish my degree? I had a work offer and would love to accept it, but the company asked me to start right now." My answer is always, "Tell them *no!*" Of course, you are allowed to start working right away without a BA or MA degree. Not everyone can afford the expensive costs of studying in a fashion school. But if you have the choice, start your studies as soon as you can, and unless you have important issues that are not compatible with this, you should finish what you start.

The professional career you will make with a degree is entirely different from the career you would make without a degree. Companies will treat you and pay you differently, especially fashion companies. If a company asks you to quit your studies, basically they are saying that they don't give a shit about you, so my suggestion is to avoid them. They are searching for a slave, not a professional to invest in. Simple as that.

Work in exchange for money or training

A common mistake among students is to accept whatever the company offers as a salary, simply because they do not know how much they should ask for. Don't work for free! Whatever you have to offer has value. It doesn't matter if that value is photocopies and coffee at first. If you're setting up a stage, the company will train you, and that training could have the same value as a master's degree. Think of the value that you are giving and the value you are receiving in return.

The fashion industry loves to hire people for free. There is a long list of companies that hire stagers for free. A stage involves training, so if they do not pay you a salary, make sure they compensate you with proper training. Training is precious! It will give you the opportunity to see behind the scenes of a fashion show, a fitting in an atelier, or the launching of a collection.

During Christmas or summer holidays, knock on doors and offer to work for free for a few weeks or a few months. Be proactive. Go to fashion week somewhere and offer to work backstage. Companies want people who are motivated. They will see that you are hungry, not there just to learn but to learn in the right way.

Start to see the value in every part of the fashion process

Even if you don't need the money, you should still try to work in the fashion industry before you finish your studies. When you receive a paycheck, you begin to gain awareness of the value of retail items, luxury items, and yourself, as a designer.

We always say to our students that in fashion school they are paying for a service, but when they join a company, they will be paid for the service. Where will that payment come from? Yes, a direct deposit into your account, but think deeper with me for a moment. If you don't understand the value of products in the fashion industry, you will struggle when it's time for you to price a product.

Money does not come from the bank. Money does not come from your credit card. Money comes from people. All the money you will receive in your life will be an exchange of a value you give. When you work in the fashion industry, you will receive money in exchange for providing value in the form of a product or a service. And there will be a person behind that amount of money deciding if what you are giving is worth their money or not.

Money is energy, and it is a simple exchange of value between people. Look at the full chain of a fashion product, all the way from the very beginning idea to the finished good being sold. There is a value contributed and a value exchanged in the form of money. If you contribute value, you will receive value in return.

Understanding of the value of things, the exchange of money, and the effort that goes into fashion products will give you an understanding of your own value as a professional. And this is something I recommend you learn as soon as possible.

Working shapes you as a designer

When I was in school, I had to go to work immediately. I was hungry to know what was on the other side. I helped with fashion shows and events. Every time there was an opportunity, I signed up. I did this partly because I had to pay for my studies, but the other part was because somehow, I knew that it would give me extra awareness about myself that would later pay tenfold.

Working gives you much more than money. It forms your attitude and builds necessary strengths that you need to learn to survive in the adult world: teamwork, working for a result and an objective, dealing with people, discipline, endurance, and so much that you simple learn on the fly. I am sure you have heard the saying "working builds a man." Well, it's true.

I also worked as a sales person in a retail store. Working part-time in a store is super useful, because you learn about the product and the client. You'll someday be designing for a client like this, and you'll know what type of products they're looking to purchase for their inventories. You'll be able to watch your clients pick up certain items, handle them, put them back down, and continue browsing. You'll see what catches your client's eye. You'll hear what questions they ask of the sales people. You'll hear the remarks they make to their friends or spouses when they're considering buying a product.

Once you have a good understanding of what type of designer you wish to be—what category of products you want to design and the segment of the market you want to design for—pursue part-time work in the stores or retailers that sell those products. For example, I worked for contemporary brands and designer labels. I avoided working for a mass market brand because I wanted more fashion-forward trends and luxury experience to learn from. However, the system has changed a lot since the 1990s when I was working and studying, and nowadays working for a well-known fast fashion retailer may give you a great understanding of the product as well, because quality standards are higher. Pay attention to the company's quality of standards. Do not compromise them when it comes to the product. If you learn about high quality, then you will design high quality.

Working in a store opens your creativity and pushes you to problem solve. One summer, I spent all of my income on clothes. The new collection arrived, and I bought as much as I could. I was supposed to use that money to buy fabric for a project, so I took two t-shirts, cut them into strips, and used them for the project. My teacher thought it was because I wanted it to use "customization" as part of the process, but in reality, I was broke and forced myself to find a solution. That solution came to me by seeing a customer using one of our t-shirts in a different way, cutting the neck and the sleeves to customize it. I took inspiration from it.

For another important luxury brand store I worked for(one of the biggest names we have at the moment), the company gave me two suits as a uniform. As I was a part-time sales assistant and was not working many hours each week, I managed to keep those beautiful uniforms in such an amazing condition that when the contract finished, they allow me to keep the suits. A few weeks later, I had one of my first interviews as a fashion designer for a brand. Guess what I was wearing for the interview? Yes, that fancy, sophisticated, elegant black suit, which I paired with a rock 'n roll vintage t-shirt from a concert. Of course, I got the job!

I had caught the Fashion Flu bug. The more I was inside that world, the more I wanted it. The best part about working in the fashion industry is that you really get to see, touch, and feel finished products. But what you don't see is the inspiration and research that went into the designs that are retailing. The method of inspiration and research will be particular to you and your style, but let's talk about how to be a truly great fashion researcher so that you'll be selling *your* brands on the shelf one day.

Chapter 9

LAST THING ABOUT SCHOOLS

Schools are not just part of the fashion system. They are also an extension of life. They are human environments where people gather together with a purpose. And as this happens, life-human dynamics happen as well. Students, teachers, board panels, directors, administrators, staff, and visitors all become part of a living organism, and all become creators of it.

People's thoughts will lead to actions, and actions will lead to dynamics, results, and behaviors. If a school has a bad environment, it's because of people in the school. The same goes for a school with a good environment: it's because of the people. I studied in three different fashion schools. The first one was full of discriminating behavior, the second was racist, and the third was extremely family-oriented. All three atmospheres were created by the people in them, not the fashion industry. The schools' cultures emerged as a reflection of how all the people in the school thought of the fashion industry.

I have taught in seven fashion schools, three of them among the best in the world. In these environments, the behaviors I have witnessed and experienced include: discrimination, fraternity, misogyny, abuse, empowerment, friendship, support, fakeness, desolation, repression, ignorance, talent, generosity, injustice, slavery, recognition, and freedom. As you see, these behaviors contrast light and darkness altogether. There is dirt where there should be beauty. And this is because as humans we have both light and darkness within us. It is our responsibility to feed the light, in ourselves and in those around us, and to turn away from the dark.

We need to focus on self-development, growth, and spirituality early on in our fashion education instead of putting all of our energy in philosophic intellectuality, just because we want to show others how deep and cool we are by developing new content, trends, books, or programs that sound fancy with lots of branding and marketing stunts. And at the end of it all, we do not give a fuck! If our behavior is making others feel abused, discriminated, oppressed, or misunderstood, our energy being poured into those fancy programs is wasted. I am talking directly to my fellow managers, directors, tutors, teachers, and students. It is our responsibility to do things right. Period.

Every time we take an action, we feel deep down inside whether it is wrong or right, and if it comes from fear or love. I may not have the answers to solve all of these problems, but I do feel the difference between what is right and what is wrong, what our responsibility is and where to draw the line. To abuse others is disgraceful, to discriminate against others is immoral, to disrespect others is contemptible, and to believe you are better than everybody else and make people feel unworthy is pathetic. Let's stop this, please. We need to focus on self-development, growth, and spirituality early on in our fashion education. We need to support designers in living full, healthy, happy lives throughout their careers.

I already feel the winds of change in our fashion industry. And it's because of people who want to improve things, people who see and understand that there are a lot of caring and sensitive souls in this industry, and schools have them as well. If you love the poetry and craft of fashion, then you love beauty, and you need to be sensitive to see all of this.

Things are changing. Things are improving. Be part of that improvement.

Let's do it together.

PART 2

Walking Blind and Doing EVERYTHING: *A Junior's Life*

Chapter 10

When you were a student, you were discovering your inner self. Now, as a junior, you are discovering your place in the fashion world. If you want to land a job that will put you on the path to great success in fashion, you'll need to show your future employers and collaborators that you know who you are. How? You need to put your personal brand into a package that has a consistent message and style. Personal branding won't happen inside classes. You brand yourself after school as you're applying for your first job. And you'll update your personal branding as you apply for every job in the future.

The first thing you need to know is that the fashion system considers a profile junior if someone has a minimum of one year and up to four years of work experience. With less than one year, you would be considered a stager (remember, going to work as a student), and after four years or more, you will be considered a senior designer. So, there is a "limbo" time of about nine months when you are not prepared to make the important career decisions but are already in the hurricane system of the fashion industry. You will constantly feel like you are learning by trial and error. You will try working for a company, pick up a project on the side, and be looking for other job opportunities, all with no clue what you are signing up for and what the job really is about. I am afraid this method of trying and erring is somewhat necessary for you to have a better understanding of the type of career you need to design.

Yes, I said *"you* need to design" because just as you will be designing projects, services, and products, you also need to design your life, including your career. Don't worry, I'm here to walk you through the process in this part of our book journey together.

The first choices we make about our career are most of the time conditioned by our ego-mind, the part of us that wants to be seen, admired, and respected. We want someone to look at what we're doing, where we're working, where we're living, and to say, "Wow, that person has it *made."* That bubbly feeling of pride? Yep, that's ego. And if you're not careful, your ego-mind will lead you into a miserable, unsustainable career. You will likely choose a brand based on the big name or the name dropping. You will choose a job based on the same standards. But by doing this, you will lose focus on the most important piece of the puzzle—the environment.

You need to understand first if what you are looking at is a painting or just a wall full of color. Zoom out, and then zoom in. If you choose the job based on the brand name, you will be focusing on the color of the wall or, what I often call, the "shiny object." You won't be paying close enough attention to understand if it is a painting of just a colorful poster. Do you see the difference? A painting has the beautiful fine brush strokes that show talent, skill, and quality. A poster *looks* like a painting, but it's flat, superficial, and cheap. Often times the luxury brand is a poster. It looks gorgeous from afar, but when you get up close, the lives of the designers inside the company are dull and lifeless. However, there is a way to choose a fashion career that is full of vibrant beauty, like a painting.

First, you begin by truly coming to know yourself, your own style, and your own desires for life. So, ask yourself the following things before you jump into your first job or project:

- In which city, state, country is the company?

- Where will I have to live? What neighborhoods?

- Is it a place that I find stimulating?

Remember, you need to do research and spark your creativity in order to produce, so the environment counts a lot! In this age, city and neighborhood research is so easy. With Google, you can find out about the city population, the country's taxes, the politics, and the social scenes. With AirBnB, you can approximate how expensive it would be to live there. With Facebook and Twitter, you can connect with people in similar shoes as you and ask what they like and don't like about the environment. All of these answers are at your fingertips, but you must first ask the right questions.

I remember that as a junior my dream brand, the designer I always hoped to work for, was located in Antwerp, Belgium.

Now, Antwerp is an amazing city, but the problem for me is the weather. I can't stand rain or foggy weather. I need the sun and warm weather. It affects my mood and my thoughts, which, in the end, will also affect my decisions and designs. This is just one obvious aspect to consider, but we often do not pay attention as we are driven by the adrenaline of working for the cool company of the moment.

You should also consider the volume of the company's business. The bigger the company, the less human the production process will be. On the other hand, in a smaller environment, the more you will have to intentionally build healthy relationships. To be transparent, the gossip can be quite overwhelming in a small company, so being able to make and keep respectful friendships will be key there.

So, which is the environment that fits you well? And here we connect with the "knowing yourself" that we discussed earlier. At beginning of my career, I thought that the main goal I had to focus on back then was learning how to be a professional designer, but I was wrong. The most important information that I was absorbing like a sponge was about how the industry works. I was not fully aware of it back then, but the year after school before I'd found my place in the fashion world was meant to train me in the dynamics of the industry: people, egos, tight schedules, demanding expectations, ups and downs, frustration, solitude, instant gratification, and the five minutes of joy after the show. It was a rollercoaster. I hated it and loved it, all at the same time.

How do you prepare for your own roller coaster as a junior in the fashion world?

Develop your personal branding

Every year, I teach both the last year undergraduates, as well as master's students, and both groups ask me the same question: "Prof, can you help me with my CV? What do I put? Who do I send it to?" My answer is always the same, "Put away the CV for the moment. First, you have to develop your personal branding."

Let me tell you what personal branding is, at least to me. This is based on my experience and what I think. Please, do not expect me to be some sort of marketing or branding guru! No, I just want to share insights I have tested and experienced myself. In creative industries, the way you present yourself is as important as what you have to offer. We live in an era where, as individuals, we all have branding-extensions of ourselves: social media, blogs, portfolios, personal images, and, yes, CVs. We have all become micro walking brands, and all the material you generate needs to be an extension of *yourself*.

Actually, everything you do is made of choices you previously made, and where there is a choice, there is intention, and where there is intention, there is you. If you create a simple CV with wide margins and standard fonts, it may be because you like to be minimalist, or it might be that you don't put effort to the things you do. Either way, the choices you make for even how your CV will look reflect who you are.

When it comes to the fashion industry, before you start working as an entry level, you need to make interviews, and to get an interview, you first have to send your CV and portfolio. You need to present yourself and what you have done in your school year to make the company understand your brand. There is a decision you need to make: how do I wish to be seen? The answer to that should be the starting point of your personal branding. The CV, LinkedIn account, or portfolio should be just a natural extension of that.

If you take care of this with intention by doing an analysis of who you are before starting to write your resume or building your portfolio in a random way, then you will start "designing" your career in a proactive way, and this will give you great results moving forward. It all begins with the awareness and understanding of who you are. Always.

There are some questions that may be helpful for starting the appropriate process of your personal branding:

In which environment do you feel most inspired?

We've talked about the importance of environment in Part 1, but figuring out your ideal environment is not only beneficial but crucial before you build your personal branding profile. Some people know this by instinct, some have forgotten, and others have still to figure it out. There are amazing authors out there you can read, listen to, and watch in order to learn about this. I am sharing with you my personal list in hopes that these are as helpful for you as they have been for me:

- *The Element* by Ken Robison

- *The Creative Pathfinder* by Mark McGuiness

- *The Little Prince* by Antoine de Saint-Exupéry

What are your talents and skills?

Now, there is always some confusion about the definitions of talent and skill. Talents are those things you are naturally good at. Skills are those you have been trained for. In some cases, both talents and skills may match, but not necessarily. You may be naturally talented in music because you have either a good sense of rhythm or a good ear. Then, you may decide to learn how to play the piano to complement this. Your talent is music. Your skill is playing the piano.

Knowing both your talents, as well as your main skills, is crucial to developing the content of your personal branding. Once you know this, all you need to do is package the content. I always say that, in fashion, the key is to be coherent with *everything*. Be coherent in the content and aesthetics of your personal branding for your success: the way you say things, the colors, the layouts, the visuals.

Think about:

- Language: whether you use straightforward words or poetic words, local slang or worldly vocabulary

- Storytelling: the stories about yourself and your art that connect with other people

- Visuals: fonts, colors, images

It should all feel like it comes from the same person.

For language, go to the library. Read authors who can describe characters and scenes. Consider classic literature, popular books, and magazines. The tone that you use in your words says so much about your personal brand. But also pay attention to how you usually express yourself. We all do it in a different way. There are people who are very poetic in everything they write and say, and then there are people who use only essential words. All of this is a reflection of your personality, and it is based on both what you have learned in life as well as your own personality.

For storytelling, take what you've learned about your preferences in language and now practice telling stories about some of the key moments in your life so far. When did you become interested in fashion? What were some of your passion projects when you were young? What were your favorite classes in school? How did you come across the inspiration for some of your favorite designs? Craft your answers into stories and practice telling them to your friends and colleagues. Whether you tell detailed, dramatic stories or short, straightforward narratives, that is your choice. And your choice is a reflection of who you are.

For visuals, look at physical mood boards using magazine and books. Create your own visual imaginarium. This is something you must be comfortable with doing already as a designer or creative thinker. We all communicate our ideas, concepts, trends, and so on with visuals. Just implement the same visual process that you would for any design work, except instead of creating for a brand or project, create a mood board that reflects your identity with visuals. The principle is the same. If you want to do digital, go to Tumblr because it's less mainstream, unlike Pinterest which is more commercial. But do not feel afraid to combine both visual material as well as tactile material. When it comes to visual research, you want to keep your head up and your eyes open to see all the possibilities.

Who are you, right now?

Create the brand for who you feel you are right now, and give yourself permission to change your personal brand over time. Your personal branding can use the art, architecture, and styles that are resonating with you now, even if it changes as you grow as a designer.

My own personal brand is an evolution, eclectic, always changing. I change the colors and fonts I'm using every few years, because the types of services and products I offer change. My visual imaginarium matches my personality: joyful, positive, driven to move forward, care for others. My old website was very essentialist: white background, with a bold, black font from the 1920s and 1930s. But I revamped the website to have a more feminine feel. In my personal life, I've embraced my own femininity, so I changed the bold font to a dark pink.

I also noticed that most of my clients, as well as students, are women. This doesn't mean that my businesses and services are just for female entrepreneurs or students, but women do make up the majority. So, I focus on developing a more feminine side of my personal branding in order to communicate better with my biggest target audience. At the moment I try to balance everything by combining my masculine side with my feminine side: 30% masculine to 70% feminine.

Do not be afraid of changing and evolving

Many people think that the CV, LinkedIn page, and portfolio need to last forever. No! All of them need to evolve together as you do. Your social media and website need to change and evolve as you do. And it is okay that you are evolving as a designer. This does not mean that you need to change things every two weeks, but every time you move forward in your career and you achieve new success and goals, make your personal branding follow them.

Change is not bad. Your personal brand and all the surrounding website and social media profiles are not decided only one time. You will craft your personal brand and rebrand. Designers are creative and interested in so many things. This is one of their biggest strengths, being obsessively interested in everything. So, of course, you need to reflect your interests in personal branding as well.

Chapter 11

Now that we are digesting the personal branding issue as something to really pay attention to in your career, especially during your early junior years, I want to share with you some tips and insights when it comes to the portfolio. Before we begin, let's first consider the foundational question: what is a portfolio? I'll tell you my personal opinion: it is a summary of all your most representative works, yes, *and* your personality, identity, and aesthetics.

Most of the material, projects, and collections you will have to show in the early stages of your career are not fully yours, because all of this work was probably made within a team. When you are a junior, you do not have permission to develop the projects and collections alone; you will be supporting the team for this, so most of the ideas within the collection, especially the core ones, are not yours. For this reason, it is important that you create material inside the portfolio that you did by *yourself* in order to show your very own personality, identity, and aesthetics. This, my friend, will be why someone will hire you, because of what *you* have to offer.

Over the years, I have helped students, entry levels designers, and senior designers to create their portfolios. For whatever reason, this is something that comes naturally to me. I love to advise and mentor, and I have a good understanding of what the industry is seeking. When it comes to the portfolio, I want to share with you the three phases mandatory to development:

1. **Content:** What to put? This is the drama! It needs to be a selection of the best and most representative works you have done so far. I always ask this question: imagine you will have the opportunity to do an interview with the designer you admire the most. Would you feel proud to show the work you selected to them? That pretty much gives you your answer. And your work should be shown in chronological order, starting with the most recent works, and should have a description just like a CV.

2. **Visual Imaginarium:** Show the way you see beauty. It's as simple as this. Show all the aesthetics you love in coherence with the content you have created. Use all the art, cinema, architecture, and literature references you are in love with. Have you noticed how often I use the word "love" here? It is because *love* is the answer. You need to FEEL in

love with the process. It is the best way to know that you are developing something right.

3. **Layouts:** How you display things is crucial to help the viewer understand you. Take inspiration from books, magazines, advertisements, and other physical artwork to better understand how to combine things in a beautiful yet powerful and clear way.

Among some of the products I create for my business are the personal branding workbooks, which I developed because peers and friends constantly request them. I decided to put all of this information in a simple yet comprehensive manual about everything I have learned to help as many people as possible achieve their goals. Here is the link to the personal branding workbook that will walk you through all of these phases, in a detailed way: http://farahlizpallaro. com/products

Your portfolio is crucial. It's a reflection and extension of you as well as your personal aesthetics. The resources you will use to refine it need to be selected accordingly. I always suggest building a bibliography of books that give you resources and inspire you for this.

You know I love books. There is always something magical about them. The book you need always seems to arrive exactly the moment you need it. So I hope my list below arrives at the perfect moment for you, my entry level junior fashion industry profile friend!

- *Papercraft: Design and Art with Paper* by Robert Klanten and Sven Ehmann

- *Content Triumph of Realization* by Rem Koolhaas and Brendan McGetrick

- *The Concise Dictionary of Dress* by Judith Clark and Adam Phillips

- *Dries Van Noten* by Pamela Golbin

- *Inkspired* by Betty Soldi

I hope these works will spark your curiosity and add to your understanding of the importance of getting inspired before developing the portfolio. Now it's your turn. Go out there, start your research, and get inspired by amazing books!

Chapter 12

YOUR PORTFOLIO HAS A SPIRITUAL SIDE

As I shared with you in the first chapter, the meaning of this book is to give you a problem-solving methodology to survive and overcome obstacles in this fashion jungle. But also, and most importantly, it's here to introduce you to spirituality and self-development as a magnificent tool to support you in this creative path you choose.

Spirituality can become the greatest support you may have in life. The amazing thing about becoming aware of spirituality is that you can apply mindfulness and all the tips we are sharing so far in both your everyday personal lives as well as your fashion world. Why? Because spirituality supports you as the beautiful light being you are in a human body experience.

So, as in all things, there is also a spiritual side to personal branding and developing your portfolio.

Alchemy

In the dictionary, alchemy is defined as "a power or process that changes or transforms something in a mysterious or impressive way." And the same is true when you are putting your creative pieces together. While developing your personal brand as an extension of yourself, your identity, your aesthetics, and your vision of things, you are creating a powerful alchemic vision of your whole *self*. And, as a result, you move emotions and thus move people.

People will react to your creation. They react to your talents, skills, and personal taste. This is truly the most hidden and the most important component in personal branding, as well as branding in general: to move people, not to convince them or pursue them, but to talk into their emotions, to talk directly and straightforwardly to their hearts.

Connection

Doing the exercise of building your personal branding connects you with your inner self. In every single step of the process, you gain more and more clarity of yourself and you connect with your spirit, which in the end connects you with the font of creation. You can call it god, love, universe, or nature, whatever you believe in. Being in connection with yourself brings you closer to the source of creation. The more you are connected with yourself, the more clarity and awareness you have from your inner-being and the better in life you will be. This is a true fact. I have experienced it. Try it, and experience it for yourself.

Open Heart Chakra

I will explain more about the importance of the chakras later in the book, but I want to start by first introducing you step-by-step to this powerful world of spirituality and self-development so that you can combine it with your life in the fashion world. For now, let's just say that when you build your personal branding, you are opening your heart chakra as well. Why does this happen? You are feeling love for yourself, and you are *expressing* love for yourself. While building things for yourself, you are giving love to yourself as well. By learning more about you and the beautiful things you are able to create, you are learning to love yourself more.

Spiritual people often emphasize the importance of having all the chakras open, and the heart chakra is key as it connects all seven chakras and at the same time it connects you with love. And you know what they say, right? Love can heal the world. I will explain more about chakras moving forward, but for now, I recommend you read *Chakra Balancing: Body, Mind & Soul* by Deepak Chopra.

Chapter 13

CHOOSING THE FIRST COMPANY YOU WORK FOR, HEART-DRIVEN VS. FEAR-DRIVEN

Now that you have transitioned from a fashion student to a designer with a personal brand and a portfolio, you are now ready for your first jobs in the industry. I was very lucky in my first working experience. I worked for a current "cult" Spanish brand that showcased in New York fashion week. I had the opportunity to work for the brand when the designer who invented the brand was still alive, and I learned *a lot* from him. It was a beautiful experience. He loved to work with young designers, and he let us create with free thinking. He allowed us to build ideas for the show, and I was on the team that was hand-making the accessories for the runway collection. Remarkably, the whole design team was very supportive, and I remember those early years with love and affection. But I didn't realize how lucky I was.

I wanted to change and move to a bigger fashion city. Madrid was not one of the mainstream fashion cities that I had wanted to live in after the first year. I was hungry for success and name-dropping, and I did not pay attention to the fact that I was extremely fortunate to start in a place with such an amazing creative environment that had allowed me to express myself as a designer from day one while at the same time learning from a master who had started his career with the Haute couture. Years later, after I'd left Madrid and this small design company, I was working in Milan for a luxury well-known brand. I had stepped into a senior position. Among the tight deadlines, high stress, and big egos, I finally realized how lucky I was with that first company in Madrid. To be honest, I wanted to go back, but I was already too far along to retrace my steps.

This is exactly why I am writing to you now when you are at the crossroads in your career decisions. Ninety-nine percent of the time, you will start your career in a place that will make you do lots of photocopies and coffee runs, filling boxes for the expeditions, supporting senior designers on everyday duties, and you will not necessarily be creating or designing as I had the opportunity to do in Madrid.

So, here are a few tips I would like to share to help you recognize those amazing places so you stick to that place like glue!

1. Do your research. Take time to investigate the company you're considering applying to. Learn about how many employees it has. Try to understand how its supply chain operates and if the company respects corporate social responsibility. Look to see whether the company has won prizes for working environments. Try to find any Facebook groups that talk of the fashion industry and what *people*—not the media or anybody else—say about that company.

2. Interview someone from the inside. Talk directly to a person who is currently or has recently worked for that brand or company. Speaking with them about their personal experiences is crucial. You can always contact people via Facebook or LinkedIn. If you have a respectful approach and tell them that you wish to know more about that company because you are considering working there, people will be open to speaking with you. You may use your network for this as well. Don't be shy about asking people you know for the small favor of a conversation. This is your career and your life we're talking about.

3. Focus on the environment. As I already mentioned, the external environment in which this company exists is as important as the internal environment of the company. The country, the city, and the neighborhood are all crucial considerations, because they will all affect your lifestyle. If you do not like the external environment, the company may be the most incredible, well-educated, stimulating brand in the world, but you will inevitably feel frustrated and unfulfilled.

Remember, your work is just a part of your life, not all of your life. It may be a very important aspect, but it is still not the whole. You need to take care of the rest of your life, too.

And let me tell you something about the companies you may find....

Heart-Driven Companies vs. Fear-Driven Companies

Two emotions move the world: love and fear. Companies are made of people, not robots (yet!). So, the human factor is everything when it comes to organizations. All of this applies to the fashion industry, as well, because behind the fancy clothes and accessories, there is an industry, a system of people. Let's not forget it. In my career, I've had the opportunity to experience these two types of companies: the heart-driven companies and the fear-driven ones. I had a chance to live both them fully. I am here to give you some insights about them so you can recognize them and make your choice according to your own desired life.

Heart-driven companies have, first of all, values. I am not talking about a simple "branding" value or a list of keywords that were designed by an amazing and well-educated marketing team that knows "how to sell." I am talking about real life values that are part of the vision and the mission of those who created the company, a leader or group of people who truly want to contribute something to this world, and the way they do it is through products and services. Their core offer to the world is most important, and they haven't forgotten it throughout the years.

These companies are concerned about product quality, respect for the environment, human rights, and wellbeing. In other words, they respect life. Some may think this does not really apply to something so superficial as the fashion industry, but you can make someone feel special, happy, and secure thanks to the product or service you are delivering.

Let me give you an example. I had a client who owned a jewelry brand, and when I asked her "Why did you choose to launch a brand?" she said, "Because I want to be independent and have success." Now, you can be independent and have success by any number of means, so this could not be the *only* motivation for launching her brand. I suggested to her that through her products, she also made many people happy! Imagine a young guy buying his girlfriend a ring to propose to her and that beautiful moment of her looking at him, holding the ring, and saying "Yes!" while tears stream down her face. That moment is possible thanks to my client's product.

Like coach and healer Jennifer McLean says, "When it comes to your business, there are three main motivators: it needs to be good for you, good for your client, and good for the world."

Here are some key characteristics of heart-driven companies:

Heart-driven companies know where they stand

They don't pretend they are curing cancer. At the end of the day, we create pants, jackets, coats, etc. These companies are very much aware of what is real and what is not. They know exactly their place in the world and how to improve it. As Marc Jacobs said, "Fashion is not something we need; fashion is something we want." And this, my friend, changes everything. Heart-driven companies are very much aware that when difficult times come, their products or services won't be requested as much as other essential products or services for society. They do not try to fake it; they are honest with their clients in every single choice they make.

Heart-driven companies are full of energy

They are bubbling with energy, but they are not fast-paced. I always laugh when I look at a job posting and among the requirements, it lists "able to work under pressure and in a fast-paced environment." What does that even mean? Am I going to work, or to war? This is a huge red flag when it comes to choosing a company. "Under pressure" and "fast pace" already tells you what you need to know!

Heart-driven companies work in an enthusiastic environment

There is speed, yes, but because people involved *believe* in the project they are building, they manage to make it their own. They take pride and make sacrifices willingly, lovingly, and eagerly. And this is not cliché. I have worked in companies like this, and I have seen projects with these characteristics. All the energy comes from the heart-driven vision and values of the people who created them.

Heart-driven companies treat people like people, not like machines

They understand the human value, they know that a person has rights, needs, feelings, and emotions, and you will see this in several different ways. First, they pay you for your work. They do not task you to work for free. Isn't it true that we all have to pay bills, that we all need money to pay for our rent, food, and cell phone; that we all need money to live?

After all these years, I really don't understand how some fashion companies convince people to work for free, just because they have a well-known brand. Stagers are the best example of this. They're usually not being paid, because the promise is that they will be trained. However, most of the time, this is a false promise, and they walk away with more knowledge about how the senior designer likes her coffee or when the creative director's dry cleaning is ready than anything about the fashion industry.

Now, a heart-driven company understands that a person needs to be paid for their work and that a company should pay someone for the value they are giving with the work. These companies understand that if you make your employees happy, they will give much more to you than what you have asked, and this will translate to profit. They understand that under-paying someone is the same concept as slavery.

These companies value your time. They do not make you work until 3am just because the ego of an art director needs to see you sit in the chair even if there is nothing to do and just to contribute to, what we would say in Italian, *ingrassare,* to fatten them up and make their egos big. In fact, heart-driven companies avoid hiring insecure art-directors specifically to avoid these completely unnecessary and inhumane working situations.

Take the qualities of heart-driven companies, think of the opposite, and there you will have a fear-driven company. Simple as that. Fear-driven companies seek just one thing....profit. Now don't get me wrong, in business profit is necessary and is a good thing, but if you chase just profit, you operate from fear. I'll tell you a secret. Ninety-nine percent of the people whose only motivation is making money at any cost will most likely lose it sooner or later, or life will pass the bill by taking away something else in exchange for all that money made with the fear motivation.

Money is energy. It is a tool of exchange. It is neither good nor bad, and because of this, it cannot be the main motivation behind a company. There must be a deeper reason for wanting to make the money. What do they hope to gain from the money? Prestige, lifestyle, respect? These are the true motivators, but their greed keeps them focused on bringing in money above all else.

Fear-driven companies show their greed by hiring people to work for them, under-paying them, and then charging an excess value for their products. The constant and unique search for profit will necessarily make them lose the main focus of the company's values. When they seek *just* profit, they compromise their values. And this will lead the brand to make choices based on the ego, while having no consideration at all for the customer or the client.

The person needs to be put first. Period. We need to create beautiful services and products in this industry for people who wish to have a better lifestyle and a more happy and fulfilled life and who seek to be surrounded by beauty. When it comes to giving the client what she or he *wants*, not needs, you have to be fully aware of the emotions that push them to make the choice to surround them with one brand's category of products and services rather than another brand's.

The fear-driven companies think they can lie to their customers by selling them in a fake way with banal marketing techniques. The heart-driven companies sell from the place of truly believing in what they offer and creating stuff that improves the lives of their community and tribe of clients— period!

When to Compromise

Early in your career, you will most likely compromise your values and take an opportunity with a fear-driven company, because you want to get ahead. Many of us do this. But this is the best way to burn out. If you want to stay in the fashion industry for the long-term, you have to match your values to the company's values. If you care about animals, you should absolutely not work for a company that uses fur and leather. You will feel completely misaligned with the products you're helping to create.

Companies create their mission and vision based on their values. Always remember that companies are made by people. In much the same way that we form friendships and close ties with other people who share our same values, we also use a company's values as to connect with the company or project.

Never forget your "why." As a business owner, the projects and clients I choose need to match the values of the services and products I sell. They need to match my personal values. When you realize that the project you are involved with has dynamics that are the opposite of what you stand for and what you believe, what for you is right, then you need to have the courage to step out and leave. Even if it may break your heart. I cannot control other people's choices or behaviors, but I can control whether I accept them, tolerate them, or reject them.

Please, never compromise what you stand for and who you are, no matter the organization or the project. Compromising your core and pushing yourself to be someone other than you is simply wrong. So wrong. We can quickly forget what is real. We forget the basis of life. We forget about ourselves, and we focus on others' expectations. We focus on the outcome, the final prize. We think everything—all the suffering, all the pain—will be worth it if we finally manage to work for that fancy brand. We think we will be happy and fulfilled if we hang with the "right" people in the industry. Let me tell you a secret: you will most likely feel miserable. I met the right ones, I hung out with them, and nothing changed. My need to be in another place remained the same.

What are your limits? Set your standards in the early stages of your career. And do not compromise them for anything. For example, if you know that you *need* to express yourself through drawing, fabrics, leathers, cutting, sewing, creation, do not compromise and enter an organization or brand that has a big name but wants you to work in a way that has no room for your creative self or does not train you in worthwhile skills.

I studied fashion design, and I wanted to be a designer and to express myself as that, especially in the early years of my professional career. I received an offer from a very well-known luxury brand. I was so excited, because I had loved the brand since forever! But the role was not as a designer. They were looking for someone to support the design team as an administrator. For a year, I became a secretary, doing tasks I'd never studied or known how to do properly. Soon, I became insecure, sad, and frustrated. I was in one of my favorite brands, yes, but doing a job that had nothing to do with me.

I do not regret that experience, because I learned so much about myself: my values, limits, and standards and that I never, ever will compromise them for any "name-dropping" super luxury fancy brand. While I don't regret my own path, I also know that you do not have to follow in those misguided footsteps. You can forge your own path and make the decisions that are best for you from the very beginning. And one of your most difficult decisions as a junior will be choosing when it's time to move to another company.

Transitioning to a Second Company

I do not know if the planets aligned or if it was karma or destiny, but I was very lucky in my second professional experience. I worked for a hip, cool Spanish brand at that time (and still is today). I loved the experience, professionally speaking. It was by far one of the most creative places I've ever been. My job as a designer was so fulfilling and joyful. I enjoyed going to work every single day. It was like *playing*! I was getting paid to *play*, as a designer. But I felt I wasn't fitting in there. I felt out of place since the very first day. I was constantly battling with myself by being super creative professionally but paying absolutely zero attention to who I was as a person, and others were struggling with how to relate to me personally as a result. So, I decide to leave and move to a different country to start from scratch in a very big fancy fashion city: Milan.

From Madrid to Milan, I left behind one home and found a new one. I was convinced this would make me feel better and help me succeed. I thought the problem was the environment and the people I worked with. I thought the problem was that I was not understood. I thought it was their problem, not mine. I thought I was a victim. But that was not true. There was no problem. In reality, I completely lacked self-awareness and had zero love for myself. So, of course, the problems were all still alive and well in Milan:

bold, present, and bigger. I left a beautiful environment for one of the most demanding, rough, intense, competitive, and selfish fashion cities in the world.

Chapter 14

SPIRITUAL TIPS FOR A JUNIOR'S LIFE

I have come to believe that there are no such things as right or wrong decisions. For years, I thought that my decision to leave Madrid and those amazing companies where I'd started my career was a very, very, *very* bad decision. The change of the environment from Madrid to Milan was shocking. Madrid had a great lifestyle with a warm and friendly atmosphere. Milan was the polar opposite. It's a city for career development and business, and while it has changed a lot since 2006 and is now way more interesting, friendly, and fun, that certainly wasn't the case back then. The environment played a big part in my struggle, especially during the first year. But I also now realize that I was very naive. I still thought that fashion was poetry, because that had been my experience Madrid.

Milan is one of the primary fashion cities in the industry. Many of the top luxury brands are located there, and I started working for them right away. The fashion industry works like the football leagues: we have first division, second division, and third division. I was leaving second division in Madrid and joining first division in Milan. I was not prepared, not only as a designer but also, and more importantly, as a person. I had no clue who I really was.

You know what they say about only realizing what you had once you lose it? Yeah, that was what it felt like. I was living in a deep, melancholic mood. Why? Because I had no idea who I was, and therefore had no idea how I was seen. The problem of not having an awareness and connection with yourself is that you have no reflection of how you are perceived from the outside. There is no alignment with the inside and outside world. And it is a terrible situation to have an identity crisis.

Lack of awareness and connection with yourself can happen at any age. Back then, because of my personal family issues, I had no clue who I was. I knew the superficial aspects of my personality, but I had no clarity on what really mattered to me, my inner calling, my soul's purpose, my persona. My relationship with my mother ended was I was 13 or 14 years old. Our lives separated then. I grew up as a woman not knowing what it meant to be a woman. I didn't have a role model to look up to and emulate. I was figuring out everything by myself. I had a close relationship with two male figures, my father and my brother, but as a woman, this was not enough.

I realize now, at 40, that back then and for most of my life, I was completely out of touch with my feminine side. I also now see that my creative side comes from my mother, as well as many other characteristics: the eye to see beauty in hard places, the sense of proportion, the harmony of colors, the balance of shapes, the love for beauty and beautiful things, and an inner way of understanding sophistication. All of these characteristics from my mother I have used in my professional career, first as a designer and later as a consultant. I have always worked in the women's side of the fashion industry, focused on women's clothes and accessories. But I didn't start creating great products until I started recalling memories of my mother and hence began to understand myself better. As I embraced my feminine side and the heritage of my mother that lives in me, things finally started falling into place.

In Milan, I had a great time professionally but a miserable time personally. For this reason, I felt myself simply disappear inside the team, allowing others to take the lead and brush me to the side. They believed I was not good enough, but that was only because I believed that I was not good enough. They treated me the same way I was treating myself. Now I see this so much more clearly, thanks to my uncovering of spiritual truths, which have truly changed my life.

The decisions we make in life are always right, because they lead us to where we need to be. Some of our decisions may be more painful than others, yes, but in the end, they all teach us and drive us to our destiny. This is the beauty of being human and having free will. That being said, I truly hope that you always choose the path of least resistance. The choices you make now may not be right or wrong, but some of them may lead you more quickly to a life of joy, happiness, and fulfillment. This is my hope for you, in sharing my story and the spiritual tips that have helped me arrive at where I am right now.

As you gain awareness of the problems that arise in your career and life, you can seek deep, spiritual help, but there are also quick tips that may help you find peace and clarity even more quickly. The depth and breadth of spiritual support that you seek should be in accordance with what your mind is prepared to understand and digest. You are no longer a fashion student. You are a junior in the industry, so I will be turning the volume up! While moving forward in each chapter as we will be passing from entry level to junior, senior, and then entrepreneur in the fashion system, your age and range of experiences will change accordingly, too, so we will continue to go deeper and wider with our spiritual discussions.

Let's begin with a foundational practice that must become a core to your lifestyle: meditation.

Meditation

Meditation is by far one of the most powerful spiritual, self-growth, mindfulness techniques available. Meditation has been practiced for thousands of years, and many ancient cultures used it in their everyday lives as a secret weapon to keep them centered, grounded, and focused. Meditation is way easier than you might think. It is simply giving yourself the right and the time to turn off all the external noise and listen to your inner wisdom. It puts you in a state of calmness and mindfulness and connects you right away with who you are, your inner light.

Starting and ending your day with a few minutes of meditation can be so powerful that you won't believe it!

I ask you to simply try it. Setting aside a few minutes of your day will not harm you, and, believe me, the results will pay you back tenfold. Download a phone app that provides guided meditation and breathing techniques. Meditate at least five minutes every day. While you're going to work, put on your headphones, open up your meditation app, and do five minutes before you walk through the front door. I use the calm.com app, but there are many out there you can try. It is so easy, simple, yet powerful.

It's important to set your mind and energy before you walk into any environment, especially in the fashion industry. You are finding your place in your environment. And, remember, you are going to a battle every single day, especially at the beginning of your career. You don't want to show up to the war out of breath and stressed. You want to walk through those front doors, calm, centered, and standing in your own power.

Protecting Your Energy

It is easy for us to become overwhelmed by the dense, aggressive energy of the other people. You've felt this before, right? Someone comes walking quickly up to you, talking loudly, waving their arms, and rolling their eyes. You can almost feel the energy draining out of you, the panic setting in. You must learn to protect your own energy when you're trying to find your place.

Try this short visualization technique when you enter a place where the energy is dense: imagine putting on your armor of white light. I picture that I have a magical watch and when I say, "Set armor on," a white light envelops me like a superhero who is suddenly invincible.

Mindfulness of the Present Moment

Practice becoming mindful of what you're doing in your body at every moment. When you were a student, you were in the craft, in your body while sewing or cutting or drawing. It was part of your training. But now, you need to excel in your craft even as you're asked to do many things in a fast-paced environment.

In this new stage of your career, you need to be in the moment as much as possible to be more productive. We all know that multitasking is a very dangerous thing. Multitasking leads you to make things in a rush and by default the quality of your task decreases. You produce more when you focus one thing at the time, and when you are a junior in a fashion organization, you will be asked to produce as much as possible. Focus your attention on this present moment because mindfulness equals productivity, as well as proactivity. Remember this always.

Even as a junior, you have the ability to influence the environment around you, wherever you are. My favorite example of this is the monkey analogy. If you have 100 monkeys and one starts performing an action, any random action, the other 99 will start doing the same thing. You can either allow the stressed, aggressive monkeys to set the tone for your environment, or you can be the intentional monkey who demonstrates mindful action. It will catch on, I promise. If you bring calm, focus, and an energy where nothing touches you emotionally, others will follow your example.

Affirmations

An affirmation is a simple yet powerful tool. All it takes is repeating an everyday statement that you create. By doing this, you reprogram your brain with a new belief. This will lead to amazing results. The important thing you need to consider is writing the proper sentence, since you will be repeating it to yourself every day. Use positive affirmations that are set in the present moment. For example, something all of us lack is self-worth. We grow up thinking we are not good enough, and so we act accordingly.

A simple and powerful affirmation you can start your days with is:

> *I am worthy.*

> *I am bold.*

> *I am more than enough.*

Choose whatever fits better for you. The power of setting affirmation with the "I am" sentences is great. You will feel and see results quickly!

We often forget how powerful our actions and behaviors are. It does not matter the role you have in the organization or how important others think you are, your actions will influence the whole as we are all connected. You may feel that because you are young, you have less influence in your company, but remember that in fashion, youth is everything. We sell the concept of youth over and over with our products, services, advertising campaigns, editorials, and shows. Seniors know that sooner or later they are on the way out. You are the next generation. People in the office are looking to you to set the tone for the next generation.

Today in the fashion industry, managers must be at least five to eight years younger than when I was a junior. You may find a head designer or a fashion coordinator in their 40s when it used to be the standard for that role to be filled by someone in their 50s. It is not required any more to have three or four decades of experience. You need experience, yes, but it is also very much required to be driven, hungry, and full of energy... *young*!

When a junior has both good technical skills and communication capacities, seniors start freaking out because they know that in two or three years, the junior will be mature enough to be competition. And if, as a junior, you're also calm and centered every day at work, you are a force!

RECAP: Your Junior Designer Spiritual Toolkit

These tips may seem simple in concept, but they are powerful in practice. Keep them in your toolkit, and use them every day. Every. Single. Day.

1. Meditate once in the morning and once at night.

2. Before you enter an aggressive or stressful situation, visualize your armor of white light so that your energy is fully, completely protected.

3. Be mindful of each and every present moment, focused on one thing.

4. Say your daily affirmations to create new positive beliefs about yourself.

And remember that even though you are young, in our industry, youth means energy, innovation, creativity, and emerging power. You are young, but you are powerful, and you can change not only your team and your company but the whole industry, if you will embrace your junior designer spiritual toolkit each and every day.

Chapter 15

BEING THE FRENCH FRIES OF YOUR DESIGN TEAM

French Fries? Let me explain. At the beginning, you are the support of the team. You are not yet the core of the team. You are not the burger. You are the French fries. And when you're eating a burger and fries, which one do you start eating first? The fries, of course. Before a request is sent to the senior of the team, it will come to you first. Juniors are often not aware of how crucial and important they are to a team as well as an organization. The support duty is crucial to maintaining balance within projects. Someone has to do the dirty job, and if no one does it, the dirty job will become overwhelming.

So, have the following in mind:

- You are not the core, but you are the crucial support within the team.

- You *are* part of the team.

- Support is essential to the project.

- You are in the perfect position to learn office strategies and politics.

You can model people who are in the core of your team. How do they do things? Why do they do them that way? You must focus on learning the successful methodology that others have crafted before you. Learn the positive things, the ones that give results. Observe people.

You need to have a clear vision of what you want to do. If you enter a place, knowing who you are, what you want to achieve during your career, what your standards are, people will not feel threatened. They'll know you're there to learn or to have your own line or to move on and become a creative director elsewhere.

Focus on your own stuff, not other people's stuff. Focus on your path and on your career and be clear about your purpose, and others will respect you. When you make it clear to people that you do not want to steal their job out from under them but want to learn from them and to create your own position in the organization, people will not feel threatened by you and will have a very different attitude toward you. Remember that because you are young, senior designers will automatically see you as fast-approaching competition. They can quickly turn on a dime and become defensive. But if you will subtly suggest that you simply want to learn because you admire them and because you want to create *new* ideas and positions within the company, they will begin to trust you a little at a time.

Success in companies is 20% skill and 80% attitude and approach. You cannot control others actions, but you have control over your reactions to them with your attitude and approach. When I was a junior at a company in Spain, I was always very clear that I wanted to have my own business and my own line and that I wasn't there to threaten others' careers in a sneaky way. In most companies, you will likely have reviews every year or so where they ask you, "What do you want to do? Are you interested in another type of product?" This is when you can be completely honest.

My father used to say "You should go to work every day as if it is the first day." Pay attention to the work itself and the quality of it. If it speaks to you, you do not have to do anything else. There is no short way up. There is no back door to creative director. You cannot skip climbing the mountain. Instead, you can enjoy the climb. Like everything in life, it is a process, and it is up to you to make it joyful!

Choices

You are a designing your career with every choice you make. The first two to three years, you have some slack because you're still learning about how you are as a designer. But still, every choice will affect the rest of your career.

Do you want to work in the luxury industry? You will need to work for luxury from the beginning. If you try mass market, then luxury, then back to mass market, you will look incoherent.

There are no random choices. Every choice affects the rest of your career. And everything happens for your higher good. So, for sure, you will be in the place you have to be and you will do what it is good for your career path. There will be errors and mistakes, but remember, we learn through mistakes, not successes.

But how do you make those first choices as a junior? Already, you must begin thinking about your "why." When I am teaching a class, I ask my students to connect with their mission in the fashion industry. I ask them to take a piece of paper and list 10 problems that they see in the fashion industry. Then, I tell them to pick ONE problem that speaks to their souls and to write out why they want to solve this problem and how as a professional they can contribute to solving this problem. This is your motivator, your "why."

I once had a student who was a stylist say, "I cannot stand companies who choose anorexic models." I said to her, "How can you change this?" She said, "As a stylist, I can request to be in the casting room and ask for models who are not anorexic." Voila! She had her why that would be her compass guiding her in deciding for and with whom she would work.

When you are struggling with the stress of the day, you will remember the reason why. You started this path not just to fulfill your single happiness but also to improve this industry as a service for others. You have a bigger mission, even if you are only beginning to understand what that might be.

My own "why" comes from the fact that I cannot stand the lack of humanity in this industry, the focus on the external but not the internal, the packaging but not the contents. So, I teach and write and speak to bring spirituality to designers. I focus first on the individual, so that individuals can then create amazing things. With everything I do, every product, service, post, article, or video I put out there, I always keep in mind my bigger why: to help improve this industry that I love by adding knowledge and combining spirituality and self-development with the whole. I am here to help create better environments, services, and products from the heart, not from the ego.

You need to start defining your bigger why, even now, in your juniors years. When you must decide where and for whom you will work and how you will interact with your environment there, please come back to this chapter and follow these simple steps.

1. Understand yourself. At this stage, you should already have at least an initial understanding of yourself as a person first and then as a designer.

2. Make sure your values match the company's values. Do not compromise your values. Make sure the company's values match yours.

3. Learn personal development and spirituality techniques. Yes, this is what we are doing here! And I hope you have already put into practice some of the spiritual tips I am giving you and are seeing the great results.

4. Explore your why. Write out why you want to solve this problem and how as a professional you can contribute to solving this problem. This is your motivation, your why.

Many people change during their junior years. They think the only way to survive is to become cynical and bitter, but this creates a snowball effect and they will burn out. If you follow this path, someday you will wake up hating the person you have become. And as Wayne Dyer used to say, in order to get what you want, "you need to first BE to then have." Be someone that other people want to be close to, not far away from. And if you are surrounded by bitterness, the best way to fight this is not by becoming bitter, but by becoming the opposite: gentle.

You will be surrounded by people who are just trying to survive. Maintain your centered self and connect with your inner self by meditating, protecting your energy, living in the moment, and working in your affirmations, each and every day.

PART 3

Strategy and Politics: Stepping Up As a Senior

Chapter 16

ARRIVING AT SUCCESS

As I mentioned to you at the start of this book, I began writing with the motivation of helping as many people as possible to overcome the struggle we have all faced in fashion to find and maintain our connection with the human aspect of this industry. In each phase of the career path for students, juniors, seniors and even entrepreneurs, the dynamics are pretty much the same. And it is so frustrating that they repeat over and over again.

As a senior, you've noticed this, right? That the same problems crop up again and again: stress, deadlines, egos, running on empty, burn out. You've been working into the evenings during the week plus weekends. You've been asked to make long business trips for three or four days and to be reachable by phone and email at all times. To make everything worse, you are treated without any sort of respect or gratitude for all the sacrifices you're making.

Now, I want you to do this. Go to the dictionary and read the meaning of "slavery." You will be surprised. I do not want you to think that I am being apocalyptic. Of course, not all environments within the fashion systems are like that. There are more and more healthy places growing. Things are changing, and we are in a sort of awakening moment. But still, 90% of the whole industry operates in a negative and abusive way. And we need to do something.

What if simple habits, awareness, and knowledge could make a huge difference? First in individual designers lives, then teams, then companies, then the whole industry? I think you, as a senior, can see this potential, can't you? We can add self-development and self-awareness in our own design lives as well as our teams and companies. We can seek to understand that before creating collections we need to focus on building healthy environments based on respect for others, mindfulness, and ethics.

For all this, I have a conviction for adding spirituality to fashion. And this is an essential part of everything I do in this industry. Fashion and spirituality go so beautifully together. You might still find yourself asking, why spirituality? To create great fashion we need to *feel,* rather than think. Thinking and understanding come later, but fulfilling creation emerges from *feeling*. You may be a manager, a senior designer, head of department, or CEO, and I know how you feel: tired, frustrated, trapped. Even with a great salary, benefits, apartment, car, designer clothes, and travel, you feel a void within you. Let me ask you this: if you are a parent, how much do you see your kids? If you are married or have a partner, how much do you see that person? And, most importantly, how much time do you have for *yourself?*

It is our responsibility to take action. We need to be the mavericks who shift this process. Hopefully, other creative industries that have similar dynamics will see the change we are creating and will find the courage to do the same. Remember the monkey analogy? We can behave in a way that will affect what 99 others around us do. You as a manager have the power to make the difference with your actions, even if you believe you don't.

And I will guide you and help you. Let me be your mentor and fashion coach.

Chapter 17

You are no longer the junior French fries. Now, you are the burger. And it'll be in your best interest to make sure you're the *meat* of the burger, not the bread or the cheese. Know how to do your job, and do it well. Do not pretend you are doing it. Mean it. Be present and conscious of it. You will have colleagues who have climbed the ladder by compromising their integrity. They may become a senior, too, but they cannot hold their position.

Be brutally honest with yourself, and know that you are ready for this role. It's not necessarily that you want to be the dress designer just because that's the most prestigious role. Fashion companies are full of hierarchy and many times seniors accept the roles and responsibilities that they think put them closer to the "kings or queens" of the companies, even if this may involve doing something they are not trained to do.

You will be tempted to take any senior role because it puts at the same table as the owner of the company, who is also often the creative director. And that person's family may be the COO and his aunt may be the CFO. All of this can transform into another shiny object that distracts you from your real path, your real contribution to the organization. In the end, remember that it does not matter how close you may be to the power. The ones who count will still treat you like shit.

So, first, you need to recognize the ego trap you've gotten yourself into. And, second, you need to find a way to operate in this position as a senior without losing your soul.

The Ego Trap

When you become a senior and you have responsibility, a good salary, and benefits, you feel like you've made it. You feel like you have everything under control. But you don't have everything under control. It's an illusion. We actually do not have *anything* under control in this life, and this is a fact. We need to learn how to *let go* of the need to control. Only by letting go of the need for control do we actually have control. When you just learn to flow and be present in the moment and know that everything that happens is for your higher good, then you have no need of control, and that is the real meaning of control, isn't it?

As a senior, you may fall into the ego trap, which lures you in with the promise of control. But soon you will be aware that it is all an illusion. They're dangling a carrot in front of you, and you're giving up your life because of your ego. You haven't made anything. You're compromising your life now more than ever. You're at the age where you should be doing things that really matter, like having family and building lifelong friendships. But you're accustomed to a high standard of living, fancy clothes, a big house, luxurious vacations, and you feel like you can never take a lower salary. Those things feed your ego. You have everything you ever wanted, but you feel miserable. There's a void inside of you, and no clothes, furniture, or vacation will ever fill that void.

When I was working at a luxury brand as a senior brand manager, I worked during all of the holidays: Easter, Christmas, New Year's Eve, and every bank holiday. As a senior, I had the budget to stay in fancy hotels, fly in business class, and eat at fancy restaurants. But what meaning does this all have if you are doing it in exchange for your precious time, especially on days that should be shared with family and loved ones?

During the Christmas season, companies always gave us gifts. The value of the gift matched our level at the company, so the juniors received small accessories and the seniors were gifted valuable products. One Christmas, I received a bag that I had been dying for. It was one of the iconic products of the brand I was working with and was made of this incredible leather. It was like nothing else in our product line and everything I wanted.

I reached for my bag, my boss smiling while saying, "Merry Christmas." I tried to smile. I held the bag, touched the leather, and looked at myself in the mirror with the bag. I felt nothing. Absolutely nothing. I thought, *"Where am I going to take this bag? I never go out. I am working all the time!"* The precious bag was just another object. I realized in that moment that you can fill your wardrobe with all the amazing, fancy, luxury objects this industry may have, but it won't mean anything if you don't have time to share beautiful moments with your loved ones. It's as simple as this.

This story is just one of hundreds of other similar stories I have heard from those seniors years in this industry, whether it's trying to fill the void with fancy objects or luxurious places. You are in deep, my friend, and you need a solution bigger than just breathing in and out slowly like I suggested to juniors. You need to make some drastic changes. Now. There is a crucial point between being ready for spiritual awakening and an expiration date. If you don't open yourself to spiritual awakening or any other self-development tool and you don't act now, you will cross over to apathy and may never return. Now is your time.

On May 22, 2009, I quit my job at a well-known luxury brand. I had the salary and the benefits, But I was dead inside. I wrote up a resignation letter, and it sat on my table four days. When I finally submitted it, Human Resources asked me why, and I said, "Do I really have to explain it to you?" It was so obvious. They know perfectly well that they push people to the limit. They create slaves. They may be wearing fancy and luxurious clothes, but they are slaves all the same. The company takes as much energy as possible from them, and when they do not need them anymore, when they are "out of fashion," they fire them.

Again, as I've said before, not all the places are same. There is a movement happening. There is an awakening process going on, and we are all in this process in the fashion world and beyond. I see positive changes in this industry that I fell in love with many years ago, but still there is so much to do, and still, the majority of behavior is based on fear and ego.

We have the great potential to bring change, and *you* can use your senior role to help improve things. Do not think there is nothing you can do, because there is! Your everyday actions, even if tiny, may make a huge difference.

Chapter 18

BECOME A STUDENT OF SPIRITUALITY

I reached the point of no return in the last period of my senior years when I finally knew that I would make a major career change. I started studying different types of spirituality. I didn't know exactly what I was looking for, but I opened my mind, simply wanting to know more about my own spiritual side. I remember during that time how I was feeling so desperate. I felt like I was in a tunnel with no light at the end. But, deep inside, I knew there was help on the way.

It arrived in the form of a Kabbalah course. The Kabbalah is an ancient spiritual study that came before Judaism, Christianity, or Islam. My friend had been a Kabbalah student for many years and occasionally brought it up to me, suggesting that I could read the book and study, too. I was hesitant about starting the course, but you know that life puts you in the spiritual path when you are ready to embrace it.

Louise Hay said, "Once I allowed spirituality enter my life, everything has been an amazing roller coaster of growth." I feel the same way. And you, too, can begin your own study of your spiritual side. It only takes an open mind and a willingness to become a student, once again. Seek the wisdom and possibilities that people have found through the ages, and there is surely one that fits you. Be open to the Universe giving you an opening to come deeper into your spiritual self.

The awakening process is so necessary when it comes to your senior years. Yes, I have already spoken to students and juniors about dipping their toes into spiritual practices, but it takes a ready mindset to embrace the full path to spiritual discovery. And when you are ready, when you have the ears to hear it, your spiritual self will speak to you.

One year on my birthday, my friend had an intuitive hit that I was finally ready. He gave me a Kabbalah book with this inscription written inside:

> "Farah,
>
> It's about time.
>
> You asked for it.
>
> —Alessandro"

So I studied the Kabbalah for almost two years. I knew that I wouldn't become a "Kabbalista" so to speak, but I simply wanted to open my mind and my spirit to other possibilities in life. I was a student again. As I turned the pages of the book, I found a new enthusiasm. To me, the Kabbalah was an abundant source of spiritual wisdom, helping me to discern what was really important in my life. I enrolled in an online course with videos, and every week I set aside a little bit of time to watch the online lectures. I started going to the meetings. They even matched me with a tutor.

I was very much interested in the teachings and wisdom of Kabbalah, not necessarily the organization or the school. But to go deeper with ancient spiritual teachings, you most likely will need to contact mentors or get in contact with centers where you can follow courses and lecturers. I want you to be careful with this. Always follow your instinct and your intuition. The wisdom of spirituality and what you learn is pure and powerful. But always remember that centers and schools are made by people, and some people have good intentions while some do not. Unfortunately, there are a lot of fanatics who use spiritual teachings to brainwash people. Choose your mentors and groups carefully. If you focus on hearing your inner wisdom with all the simple yet powerful techniques we've been talking, you will always be in balance. And you will see from a distance who has bad intentions.

Since I first started studying the Kabbalah, I have been intentionally testing the learnings. I remember the moment I read one line: "Do not be reactive. Be proactive." I happened to be on a trip to Paris for a research trip. The flight was canceled, which was a big drama, and there was a line of people yelling. I remember thinking, "Farah, let's apply this. Let's see if this works. Okay, fine, I'm going to sit here and let it flow. I'm going to lean back. I'm not going to be *reactive*. Instead, I will be *proactive* and see all the positive aspects of that situation."

If you have ever found yourself in a similar situation, then you know how hard it is to keep from becoming frustrated and upset! I reminded myself that if I am in this situation there must be a meaning for it, even if I do not see it now. A lady from the airline company approached me and said, "You're a frequent flyer, right? And you're going to Milan? We can book you on the next flight. Economy is overbooked, but we have open seats in business class." You can imagine the big smile I had on my face.

The results are real. It's not just about reading a book. It's about committing to becoming a student to a new way of thinking, being, and experiencing the world. Your goal is to upgrade yourself, to grow yourself. Motivation makes time. As a senior, you are ready to explore your spiritual life more deeply. Do not be afraid to commit and follow any spiritual studies of your choice. Pick the one that resonates more with you, and do it. It will change your life. It will change the way you see, envision, and experience the world.

Chapter 19

YOUR BIOLOGICAL NEED FOR LIFE-WORK BALANCE

Did you catch that? That's right—life-work balance, not the other way around. You need to have a life first to have work balance! You give so much time and energy to the job. Plus, you are convinced you will "make it," that once you develop your career, everything will fall into place. You give, give, and give, and you don't get any of those things in return. Maybe you've been single for many years, because you've been giving everything you have to the job. I do not want to sound disrespectful. Believe me, I am in the same boat as you. I've been single for many years, especially during my senior years in the fashion industry. No one wants to be in a relationship with someone who works on the weekends and holidays, travels all the time, and finish every night around 9pm or 10pm if you're lucky. There's a saying in the industry: if you are in a relationship when you enter fashion, it won't last long!

You may not have even thought about life-work balance until this phase. While you were a student and a junior, you were in your 20s, you had energy and drive and had distant dreams of building a family. But now you are a senior, maybe in your mid-30s or 40s, and even if you still have energy and drive, you have less to pull from. Your life goals have changed. You start questioning how you use your time. You start wanting to share your life experiences with someone. You start wondering what you are going to leave in this world, what legacy, whether that's kids or a cause or something else, something *yours*.

This is certainly true for women, but it's also true that the need to achieve life-work balance is not just related to being a woman and having the biological clock going tick-tock and pushing you to do something about it. It also applies to men. If you are reading this and you are a man, you may feel the same way, that in your 30s or 40s life you are adult enough to want to have a life project with someone. By now you should have had all the fun and dates you wanted, but now the biological need to settle down may appear on the horizon.

I am being generic here, of course. We all know people who are in their 40s but still want to have a lifestyle of a 20-year-old, and this is perfectly fine. My point is that you need to have *time* to have fun as well, right? All of us need to achieve the life-work balance as soon as possible. Some people think that achieving this is an illusion. I don't. I think is hard, yes, but it is possible as well as necessary. But the question is, how? These practical tips may help you to bring more *life* back into your daily existence:

1. Learn to put boundaries on your time

This is, by far, one of the most difficult things, especially when it comes to work. I think we need to learn to say "no" even as a junior, but, of course, you may not have felt that this was possible in that moment. You were focusing on finding your place in the working environment, so you most likely felt the pressure to be elastic and at the team's disposal. You are a senior now. You need to avoid to become a "yes woman" or a "yes man," the type of manager who always says yes to the company, because you are afraid to stand for your own values. This is so wrong. You need to create limits. Sometimes when you say "yes" as an employee, you are at the same time saying "no" to yourself as a person.

The fact that you work for them does not allow them to take your power away. In fact, there is no such thing as people taking your power from you. You *give away* your power by giving up your free time, your personal space, your private life, and so on. So please, please, learn as soon as possible to say "no" to unnecessary and disrespectful requests. I know what you are saying now: "Easier said than done!" Yes, you are right! But have you ever *tried* it? Start by practicing saying no to small tasks and requests. I promise that it will be the first step to you setting boundaries that will make room for life.

2. Learn to prioritize

Prioritize everything: task, duties, people, all areas of your life. Prioritize both what you prefer to do as well as what is really necessary. We often lose our day to unnecessary tasks. We start out answering emails and then are drawn quickly into the digital trap. As a senior, prioritize research in order to nurture yourself, because your ideas are going to be the ones developed by the company and are crucial for every creative role.

The key is to give your best time and effort to what you like to do most. If it is drawing, organize your team so you can have more time in the drawing creative process than in the management and bureaucratic one. There are plenty of books about learning how to prioritize in life, as well as videos on YouTube. Listen to Tony Robbins and you will be amazed by how many easy techniques you can implement in your everyday tasks.

3. Pause and reset

At certain points in our life, we should all hit the pause and reset button. Pausing and resetting is an incredibly healing process. We tend to hold onto things—past hurts, regrets, expectations—and are designed to hold onto things in order to persevere nature and life, especially as women. And companies are aware of this. Have you noticed that in fashion companies, there are some management roles that are 90% of the time led by women, including product managers, atelier managers, fashion coordinators, buyers, and merchandisers? The reason is simple: because companies need people to commit years to this type of role in order to avoid turn over effect, and they know women will do this.

I encourage you to question everything that you've committed to, especially in your senior years. Make a list of pros and cons. Evaluate yourself and your situation. You know those yearly revisions corporations send to their employees? Well, you should do the same with yourself. How many of your values have you compromised for that job? Be honest with yourself. I know the answer may be brutal. I 've been there, too. It is hard, yes , but necessary to wake yourself up from the ego trap.

4. Make habits of mental and physical health

Will Smith shared in an interview once that he reads and runs every day. I love this idea, because it means you are doing something mental and physical every day. Of course, choose what fits for you best. But the point is to create a healthy daily habit that will benefit you mentally and physically. I incorporate daily spiritual practices like meditation and gratitude during my mornings and evenings, and I walk every day. As much as possible, I avoid taking the car, bus, or train, because walking gives me peace. I make sure I have plenty of time during the day to walk around with my beautiful dog, Gary.

Make your own healthy daily habits to re-balance your life. Explore as many things as possible at first, and then settle on what fits best for you. Remember, you are not a robot! You are an amazing light being having a human experience.

Chapter 20

DECISION FATIGUE

I first heard the term "decision fatigue" in an interview with Jim Kwik, a world-renowned expert in optimal brain performance, and the term resonated with me right away. I thought to myself, "Wow, that is *exactly* what happens in the fashion industry with senior management." As a senior, you are constantly asked to make decisions, both small and big. And most likely you will find yourself giving the same energy to both, even if you are not aware that you are doing so. But your soul, mind, and body are amazing, and your subconscious mind—which is the real pilot and captain of your life—will make decisions for you even if you are not aware of it.

When your inner you realizes you are arriving at the limit of your resources, because you have pushed yourself too much, your subconscious will choose the path of least resistance. This may not be the path you *want*. Maybe you will accidentally eat a fast, unhealthy lunch because it feels like the least resistance at that moment. Maybe you will skip your exercise every day this week because it feels like the least resistance. Maybe you will cancel that night out with a friend because you're just looking for an evening of least resistance. And then the next week, you wonder what happened to the life you wanted.

It's because you got tired of making decisions. So, how do successful people make decisions that are good for their work *and* good for their lives? Let's use an example that fits perfectly with the fashion industry: the choice of what you wear. As Jim Kwik pointed out during the interview, the most successful entrepreneurs out there always wear the same type of looks and clothes. If you remember the amazing Steve Jobs, he always wore a black turtleneck and jeans every day. Mark Zuckerberg from Facebook wears plain t-shirts and jeans every day. These people make huge decisions that affect society and the global economy, so they choose to focus their energy on the important decisions, *not the small ones.*

I know what you are saying at this moment. "Wait, but what you wear is so important in fashion!" And yes, it is true. So, now, I have a question for you: why do most of the managers and seniors of the fashion industry choose to wear black? It is not just because they think they look thinner! Buyers wear black. Senior designers wear black. Directors and coordinators of fashion schools wear black. And the list goes on and on. Some do it because the rest do it and they think it is cool (remember the monkey analogy?). But some do it in an intuitive way, because it is the path of least resistance.

I have a controversial perspective. (You are not surprised, are you?) I reject the idea of needing to wear total black as a fashion uniform. It's not that I do not like black—as a matter of fact, I think it is an amazing color—but I think you should toss it. Because wearing the color black *kills your aura!* And, my friend, your aura is such an important thing.

Your aura is not a hippy-yuyu concept! It is the energy level that surrounds your body. If you speak with any engineer in physics, they will tell you that everything, absolutely everything in this world, is made up of energy. We are like walking batteries. And black is a color that covers. In the same way that it makes you look thinner, it also makes your energy disappear. This is most likely why you wear black in the first place. It makes you less noticeable. It covers you up. It covers your *light.* But to attract the best in your life, you have to shine and allow your body energy to react with the environment. Why do you think yogis wear all white? For the exact same reason that insecure people wear black. While insecure people want to disconnect from it all, yogis want to be as connected as possible with the environment.

Of course, I am not telling you *not* to wear black. I am telling you to avoid covering yourself with layers and layers of black because you wish to disappear, do not want to stand out, or feel you need to do what others do to belong. I know many people will consider this stance taboo, because you cannot touch the black dress code. But I believe that you can create in a mindful way your own personal style that reflects your values and what you stand for, and create a uniform from that. By wearing the same outfits every day, you will have one fewer decision to make. And, yes, you can wear some black.

Chapter 21

Panic attacks are the first warning signs of anxiety and high levels of stress. They are incredibly common in seniors and the fashion industry. Stress is the illness of the 21st century, and I have found this to be so true in our fashion world. But how do we typically deal with stress in creative industries? We don't. We avoid the problem pretend it does not exist.

So what we do in order to feel less stressed? If anything, we take drugs, legal or otherwise. I have a friend who is doing very courageous work in the fashion industry by pointing out all the mental health problems. It is a sad fact that most talented designers have committed suicide, either intentionally or accidentally by overdosing. I don't think I need to say names, right? The history of fashion is full of talented people who cannot deal with the stress, addictions, and their own personal issues.

I'm not qualified to discuss illegal drug use, but, as I have been doing since the beginning of this book, I will speak honestly with you about the consumption of legal drugs within the fashion industry. This is something I turned to during my own senior years. Many of us drug ourselves every day to go to work. We may take all kinds of pharmaceuticals, from the light ones to the hard ones. Every now and then, especially under meetings and collections, I had to take Lexotan, a sedative that helps with panic attacks and anxiety. Other people I have known took Prozac or other antidepressants. These are perfectly legal, but we should ask ourselves, what is causing us such anxiety and depression?

I remember when I went to the doctor the first time after a panic attack. It was the last day of work before the summer holidays. I received a phone call from the fashion coordinator of the company, who yelled at me for a problem we had with a supplier. She said that the supplier made a mistake in ordering a shipment of embroideries, so the collection would be delayed. She said it was my responsibility and that I had to respond to the issue by paying for all the delays and expenses out of my own pocket. After I hung up the phone, my vision was blurry. I couldn't breathe. A guy crossing the street actually came over to me to hold me up by the shoulders since it was clear I was about to faint. Thank God I was close my doctor's office. My head was in pain, and I literally thought I was about to die. As soon as I arrived at the office, the doctor put a pill under my tongue. It was the same pill they give people who are having a heart attack.

This happened in late July. I gave my resignation in late May of the following year, which means it took me almost a year to find the courage to get away from that unhealthy environment. I do not want you to do the same thing. I want you to proactive. Do not give your precious time and life to companies like this, just because it is one of the most important luxury brands in the world. The panic attacks usually happen like this. First, you push yourself to the limit. Your heart starts pumping fast. You can't breathe. You might faint. You literally feel like you are dying. This is what happened to me. More than once. What do you do? You go to the doctor, of course, and the doctor suggests you leave that job and get more rest. But you are so stuck in the wheel, essentially suffering from Stockholm Syndrome, and you adamantly say, "No, I can't leave!" So, the doctor prescribes a week at home to rest, as well as some Lexotan to help you survive the pressure and overcome everyday challenges without going into a full-on panic attack. If you are lucky and you find a good doctor, they may also refer you to a psychologist.

But, please hear this, loud and clear, when you arrive at the panic attack level, this is your *big red flag*. Do not think that you can overcome panic attacks by taking drugs. Do not fool yourself that after the collection launches, everything will be better. You know it won't. Stop lying to yourself. Plus, do you want to take drugs forever when you are just in your mid-30s? There are many solutions. And one solution is to embrace the spiritual path and deepen your self-development. Use these two amazing tools to connect to what it is *really* important in life!

Here's the honest, harsh truth. If you don't do something, if you choose to avoid the problem, you will experience intense apathy. And you will not come back from apathy. Apathy usually comes in the form of an emotion-numbing array of drugs and the initial stages of depression. I have friends who gave another five years to a company they simply didn't care about, to a job they hated, to an unhealthy environment, all because they fell into apathy. The sad thing is that no one is going to give them back those five years they spent doing the same thing every day feeling empty and unfulfilled. As a matter of fact, I know people who are still in those companies, and it has been 20 years. *Twenty!*

Don't get me wrong. It is *your* choice to give all your professional career years to one company if you wish. I personally think times have changed and this tradition belongs more to the generation of our parents. But, if the company is the perfect place for you and you feel like you can evolve, grow, and express yourself there, then great! I am talking to you, the senior manager who wants to run away and sees no way out because you feel trapped.

Do you want off your meds and finally living a healthier, calmer, more relaxed life, whatever company you are working for? Good. Let's talk about your senior spiritual toolkit and the tricks you can keep up your sleeve to prevent panic attacks and apathy altogether.

Chapter 22

There is a theory called the Three Times Rule that says for everything you put out in the world, it will eventually come back to you three times fold. If you put love out there, you will receive three times the love back. And if you put fear out in the world, well, you know what you will be receiving three times back! We attract what we focus on. We are lamps that interact with the world that surround us, and the type of light we emit influences the forces we attract.

I've been thinking a lot about this chapter. Before writing it, I wanted to make sure I prepared the right set of tools for you to use in your spiritual and self-development path, tools that I have tested myself. Honesty has been key for me since I first started writing this book. Again, I am not a guru or a spiritual master; I am in the process of learning just as you are. From everything that I have tried, three techniques have proven to be essential to my own development: *Law of Attraction, visualizations, and meridian tapping.*

These three tips, together with the studies of any spiritual teachings you choose, will help you grow, evolve, and become a better version of yourself. You will for sure have a better understanding of who you really are and what you are meant to do in this lifetime. Plus, they will help you become a co-creator of your life. There are many people in this world who have no idea how much power they hold. They are not aware that we create our reality through our emotions, feelings, and thoughts that in turn lead to our actions. There are some direct choices that create our lives, and there are some indirect ones that we are not fully aware of in the moment. We are the source of these choices.

I would like to share a quote from the amazing Susan Ferraro, intuitive coach and healer, who says, "Life does not happen TO us, life does not happen FOR us, life happens FROM us."

She is amazing, and I encourage you to check out her website: susanf.com for videos and articles that explain more fully her perspective on how we are powerful co-creators of our lives. Susan had a successful career in the fashion industry but one day she realized she felt miserable. Thus, her awakening process began, and she reconnected with herself and took the courage to embrace her calling. I mention Susan to you as an introduction to the first tool I want to share with you.

Law of Attraction

I am sure you have heard about this one, right? There was a movie years ago called *The Secret*, and there is also a book, of course. I recommend you see the movie and read the book but also try to do more research about it. *The Law of Attraction: The Basics of the Teachings of Abraham* by Esther and Jerry Hicks is another good place to start. Again, Susan Ferraro will be super useful, since she has been using this powerful tool all her life.

In simple terms, Law of Attraction explains that we attract what we are. If you feel abundance, you will attract abundance. If you feel lacking, you will attract lack. It all begins from within you. Of course, it is more involved than this, and there some steps you need to learn and master to properly use the Law of Attraction to your advantage. But remember, it is a powerful tool, which means it can backfire on you.

Where you focus, it expands, so if you focus on what you want but do not have at present, you will attract more of that. If you focus on the fact that you do not have it, you will attract even more lack. Get it? For this reason, before you use Law of Attraction, you need to learn to be grateful every day so that you will attract more of that in your life. The important thing from my experience when it comes to Law of Attraction is that you have to feel "aligned" internally with your thoughts, emotions, feelings, and desires. When all of these are conveyed into a unique, powerful intention, then, my friend, magic happens.

I recently moved from Milan to Florence and had to go through the apartment hunting process. I wanted it to be a beautiful home in a great a charismatic area of the city that did not cost me a fortune. In Italy, homes can be expensive, especially apartments, because of down payments and bureaucracy. From the beginning, I was so much in love with my choice to move to Florence. My intentions with everything that had to do with Florence were full of love. So

I unknowingly aligned my emotions, feelings, and thoughts surrounding the home I wanted to live in.

I saw just two houses in Florence, and today I live in the second house that I saw. It came to me through a friend of a friend, and it is a beautiful, gorgeous home on one of the best streets in town. The home had belonged to two architects. Because we had a common friend, they offered me a better price and contracts in my favor. See? You do not have to know ahead of time or figure out how this will happen. Leave this to the universe. The universe is way smarter than we are.

Your job is to align yourself with love and intention.

Visualizations

If you don't know how to do visualizations, you will attract the wrong thing. This is important for you understand. There is a reason why I only recommend visualizations to my senior friends. Lots of people encourage daily visualizations during meditation or before going to sleep, but it can be very risky if you don't have a clear vision of what you want. Remember what they say: be careful what you wish as it may come to you. It is totally true, and it happens often with visualizations.

First, make sure you visualize just the positive things you want in your life. I know it sounds stupid, but you can't imagine how many people visualize bad things happening, and one day those bad things become real.

A personal tool I use to make sure that my visualizations match what I want to attract into my life is creating a mood board. As a designer, this will sound familiar to you. We do mood boards all the time at work, so you will find this familiar and comfortable. The process of mood boarding implies editing, as you know. So, while choosing the images to create your board, you will gain clarity on what you really want. After you create your vision board or mood board, make sure you put it in a place where you can see it before you go to sleep and when you wake up, so you can visualize all the images of what you wish to attract into your life.

Second, make sure you feel the emotions of living in those things on your mood board. For example, if you put an image of a beautiful car, when you visualize it, imagine how it will feel being inside the car: the smells, the sounds, the emotions. I know sometimes it may be difficult, as your mind will play tricks on you. Remember, as Alan Watts says, the mind is like a monkey; it jumps up and down!

So, to avoid this, you may find the next tip useful.

Meridian Tapping

Meridian tapping is an amazing technique that combines affirmations with acupuncture pressure to send messages to your brain. While you say positive affirmations, you press with two fingers on specific points on your head, neck, and arm that will help you rewire your brain and clear limiting beliefs.

I am explaining this technique to you in a very simplistic way, so I encourage you to find information on YouTube where there are some amazing videos about it. I personally follow Brad Yates—he is amazing! He has hundreds of free videos on YouTube as well as courses on his website that will help you learn how to use meridian tapping. I personally use it when I feel stressed or overwhelmed and need to calm down. After I am in a calm state, I can focus on my visualizations and use Law of Attraction.

Remember always that we are our worst enemy, and the limiting beliefs about ourselves that we have been carrying since we were kids can prevent us from having positive results with the other spiritual tools I recommend you try.

RECAP: Your Senior Designer Spiritual Toolkit

Keep these tips in your toolkit, go deeper into studying them, and use them every day.

1. Use the Law of Attraction in your favor by aligning with love and intention and focusing on what you want to bring more of into your life.

2. Visualize the life you want—what it feels like, smells like, and looks like.

3. Practice meridian tapping when you are feeling stressed or anxious.

Chapter 23

THE UNIVERSE PROVIDES,
ALWAYS

Remember when I submitted my resignation letter? I had no Plan B, no interviews planned, no nothing. But three days after I quit, I received a call from a friend in London who was calling me about a job. He offered me the position of trend researcher for the Italian market for one of the top digital trend research agencies. I ended up loving that job. I collaborated with the agency for almost three years, and it was an amazing experience working in the field of cool hunting and trend research.

Thus, my freelance career began. And it was exactly what I needed. I discovered that I have a more entrepreneurial mindset than an employee's mindset. It is not that one is better than the other, they are just different and you need to take the path that fits best for you. To me, freelancing felt like what I had been searching for in my professional career since the beginning. I like to lead. I like to give results. I like that it's up to me to achieve those things. I need freedom to give my best. And I love to be my own boss, even if it may be lonely at times.

So I quit my job, and one week later, I already had a client. I loved it, because it allowed me to express myself much better than I ever could as a designer. Every time I had the guts to jump without a net, following my intuition and my inner self, I succeeded. The Universe, God, Nature, whatever you want to call it, is there for you. If you choose from the heart and follow your mission, it will help you all the way. It always does, even in the small decisions, nudging you on toward your life's path. Simply look for the signs. Ask for the signs.

Every time I leave my comfort zone and follow my intuition or my heart, the Universe provides and gives me signals all the way. And you will be surprised by what is on your path! Like me, I am writing a book. WOW! I would never have dreamed of doing something like this. I never planned to be an author. But I choose to write a book to help others overcome the same difficulties I endured in this fashion industry by introducing the wonderful path of spirituality and self-development.

And because I am doing this from the heart and for you, my amazing reader, I am sure the Universe will provide me with all I need to overcome my fears in the process and will bring this book to the people in the industry who are in need of it. You know what they say, faith moves mountains. There is a bigger plan for all of us, and you may feel the cosmic support in yours when you have the courage to stop following the status-quo and follow your life mission. Always have faith.

Think of humanity as a well-designed spider net. All of us are connected with amazingly strong, thin silver threads. If you place yourself in the right position of the net, the threads will stretch and move in harmony. If you are not in the place you are supposed to be, the threads will break or fold and create knots. We all have to move fluidly. Being connected and centered in the place that was designed for us will touch another person, and then another, and then another. We are all pieces of light, part of a bigger universal fountain that we call "God."

I know, I know, I'm being very spiritual here, but you are a senior now, so you are ready for this! And you are ready to think about changing your life and choosing a new direction, one that will bring you joy, satisfaction, and peace. Can you imagine? ;)

PART 4

Changing Life:
Choosing A New Direction

Chapter 24

THE LIFE YOU LIVE IS
YOUR CHOICE

Something is shifting inside of you, isn't it? You may be deciding to approach your role at your company differently, or you may even be about to make the choice of leaving the comfort of working in a fashion company to step into the unknown. I'll help to make it simple for you. Your best alternatives to being a senior designer at a brand are to 1) leave the industry entirely or 2) continue in it as freelance or a business owner.

If you choose the first one, you can leave behind the fashion industry altogether and start over in a new industry. And this is very common in fashion. I know people who left super well-known fashion companies to open a bar or a pizzeria! Often in the industry, we joke about the idea of opening a spa or a bed and breakfast, and many people do exactly this after 15 or 20 years. Some become a coach or a counselor. After all, designers have lived through some major drama and now have a good perspective on how to manage conflict. They study and train to become healers as they have the urge to help others recover from the suffering in this industry.

But there is a group of us that battles with the love/hate of this industry. We have the fashion bug, and though I can't really explain what it is that drives this feeling, I know it is not one single thing but many small things together that push us to continue working in this industry. We choose it based on passion, and it is still very present inside of us. When you arrive at this level, and you feel still love for this industry, you want to contribute to healing it from the inside. And freelancing, at least at first, helps. Since freelancers still work in the design industry but on their own terms, this is the best first baby step, and I encourage you to consider this. The first years of being a freelancer (or consultant) are very difficult, because you need to chase jobs and opportunities, literally. But as the months pass, you start to build your network and more opportunities present themselves.

The best part of being a freelancer is when you are still relatively unknown, you have the right balance of work opportunities and free time. And the most important part of being a freelancer is your freedom! You are your own boss. You decide when to work and how to work. And this is what I love most. Plus, as I mentioned, you have the opportunity to contribute to improving this industry with a different methodology that you can apply with your clients and to your projects.

But, at one point, it all may become pretty overwhelming. After five years, you start gaining recognition and become more well known. Your happy clients will tell their colleagues, and offers will really start to roll in. The thing is that you are one person, and the client wants you. You can have as many assistants as you want, but the client will still want you in meetings. With this comes the mindset problem. If you are not prepared to be a business, a consulting *firm* and not just a solo consultant, then the influx of business will be hard for you to deal with. What you struggle most with is realizing that at one point you start to compromise your freedom. You have so many responsibilities that you find yourself working on weekends and holidays, just like you were in your slavery full-time job. Freedom becomes an illusion. And you suddenly realize, "Okay, so here I am again, having no life as it used to be as a senior in the fashion companies. How do I get myself out of this?"

As consultants, we are always afraid to say no to a project, because we never know what is going to come next, if we will have more opportunities on the horizon. And this is also a trap. You may fall into the "lack mentality," and it is the worst thing that you can do. When you find yourself in this situation, it is mandatory that you make a habit of doing a checklist every now and then, and remind yourself of the reasons you chose this career path, this project, and this lifestyle. In these moments, remember to tap into your abundance mindset and choose to believe that jobs and projects will flow to you. Jobs, projects, and money come from people. Running your own design consulting business is as simple as an exchange of value, and there is always more value so long as you can balance the projects coming in and the work coming out in a sane way.

You have spent most of your career as a victim, but now you are stepping into a battle with yourself. There's nowhere to hide. You will be the one blocking yourself. If you choose to be a consultant, do not compromise your freedom. You will still have to take care to not fall into bad old habits and dynamics that you already know from your past employee life because, as you know, this industry can easily draw you back into the same broken system.

To avoid creating your own enslaving design consulting business, you'll need to develop the right mindset as soon as possible. Mindset is an enormous topic and is deeply tied to the path of spirituality, which I plan to talk more about in my next book for fashion consultants and entrepreneurs.

Chapter 25

LACK MINDSET VS. ABUNDANCE MINDSET

I'd like to ask you to answer this question honestly: do you see the bottle as full or empty? Or do you simply see a bottle with liquid inside? How you *choose* to see the bottle makes a huge difference in your life. I emphasize "*choose*" because, yes, it is always your choice. As I said before, what you focus on expands. If you focus on what you do not have, you will have more feelings of lack, not having what you want, and striving for more. But, if you focus on what you *do* have, you will have more feelings of gratitude, having what you want, and feeling content with life.

To have an abundance mindset is to always—and no matter what—focus on what you do have and to be grateful for it. Cultivating an abundance mindset is crucial for working as a freelancer or as a business owner. Why? When you focus on the projects, work, and clients that you *do* have, you will get *more* projects, work, and clients. When you have done all your homework, have built your network and personal branding, have gained awareness of your talents, and have developed your skills (which you did all along your path as a junior designer and a senior designer, right?), then you have nothing to worry about. Nothing at all. You must be absolutely confident that offers will come to you. However, if you cultivate a lack mentality—focusing on the clients you *don't* have, the money you *aren't* making, the projects you *aren't* landing—then you will block the flow to your business.

When I started as a freelancer, I always knew I had a lot of value to offer to my clients. I knew I had the knowledge, talent, and skill to serve them and to help them achieve their goals. I had an abundance mindset. For this reason, I had clients come to me right away. The first year, of course, I let the market know that I was available as a consultant, but after that year I never chased a client because opportunities came to me, always. This was partly because I had created a very extensive network throughout my years as a designer for other companies and partly because my work (my personal brand!) speaks for me. But, I will tell you, my success has also been because I have developed and continue to maintain my abundance mindset, day in and day out.

But I also know the other side of the coin and how it feels to have a lack mindset in other areas of my life, like the personal ones. And I do struggle with my own lack mindset, even today, around relationships and love. It is a constant battle with myself, but I am aware it is just my mindset and by *choosing* to change my mindset, I can be successful in any facet of my life, whether that's business or relationships or love. It is important to recognize your shadows so you can open the windows and allow the light to come in.

How do you build an abundance mindset? Train your mind, and feed it regularly. All of the spiritual tips I have given you so far will help you to do this, but now you are ready for more, for deeper training in spirituality. Let me give you a few more tools, so that you can choose your abundant mindset.

1. Feed your mind with the right information

You have the power to choose what to hear, read, and see. I can tell you for sure that among the most successful people in the world, many of them do not have a TV. Why? They choose to select the type of information they feed their brain. They do not want to leave this choice to a TV channel. Be very picky with what type of information you allow into your life, as it makes a difference in what you focus on every day.

2. Surround yourself with motivators and winners

Seek out people who choose to be leaders of their lives, not victims. Discreetly avoid people who always find problems in everything rather than potential solutions. Don't get me wrong, we all need some discomfort and feel miserable every now and then, but I am talking about all those people who love to be a victim and always complain because that way they have all the attention and sympathy. Our choices are conditions from the people that surround us, even if we are not aware of it.

3. Take care of yourself

Always, and no matter what, take care of yourself mentally and physically. If you do not take care of yourself, no one is going to do it for you. You may have support from others at times, but taking care of yourself is your responsibility. Remember that when you are in a place of abundance, of good health mentally and physically, then you are in a position to give to others.

I encourage you to write down your priorities, and soon you will see that the lens through which you see your life and the world, in general, will change. When you start waking up each morning with a smile and going to bed at night also with a smile, you will make it. There will be days that will be hard to do so, but I tell you it is possible. I have tested it myself, and I have complete faith in you that you will find the change you are looking for, my friend.

I could give you more spirituality tips for your entrepreneurial life (and I will in my next book!), but for now I want you to develop your own path based on your priorities and your own life.

Chapter 26

DEAR ENTREPRENEUR, DO YOU NEED SPIRITUAL TIPS?

Well, of course, you do! Spiritual tips are your magic wand when it comes to dealing with this crazy and chaotic fashion industry as an entrepreneur. At this stage, I assume that you know some of the *basics* of spirituality and self-development. You probably have endured at least one difficulty in your life that made you stop and reflect on what it is really important and what is not.

I still encourage you to review all we have discussed so far in this book, to create a list of the tips and suggestions we have discussed, and to check which ones you may or may not know and which ones you wish to try. After you do this, you will graduate to the next step, the master's degree of your spiritual toolkit.

Ready?

Family Constellations

This is the only tip I have for you, my freelance and entrepreneur friend. But it is a powerful one. Before I explain to you why, let me share with you what Wikipedia says about Family Constellations:

> *Family Constellations, also known as Systemic Constellations and Systemic Family Constellations, is an <u>alternative</u> therapeutic method which draws on elements of family systems therapy, <u>existential</u> <u>phenomenology</u> and <u>Zulu</u> attitudes to family. In a single session, a Family Constellation...reveal[s] a previously unrecognized systemic dynamic that spans multiple generations in a given family and to resolve the deleterious effects of that dynamic by encouraging the subject to encounter representatives of the past and accept the factual reality of the past.*

The power of this therapy is incredible, and it will change you forever. The benefits and effects of it will last years and years.

The companies you work for often end up being a replica of family systems. Your boss becomes your dad, the older female employee becomes your mom, and the coworkers your age become your siblings. I am always amazed by how we tend to personalize the characteristics of our family members in our coworkers. In the school where I teach, some people react to the director as if he were their father. In one of my client's companies, the business owner and art director "mothers" the team. It is more than just business, because there are family dynamics involved, always.

Our families are the first business organizations we know, so when we go to build and work for other systems, we tend to recreate the first dynamics of human interaction we know, and these are the ones with our families. Think about it: do you often expect to be treated in a specific way in the company you work because it is familiar to you? And now reflect a moment on why we call this "familiar"? Because it comes from our family. (There's a reason they share the same etymology).

Now, when we talk about unhealthy environments in the fashion industry, of course, this happens because of the human dynamics and systems that have been created inside the organization. There is often a lot of drama, because people bring their own personal drama into the office. If you haven't discovered, healed from, or gained an understanding of what type of healthy or unhealthy relationships you have with your parents, relatives, and ancestors, your life will be conditioned by actions and behaviors that most likely you are just replicating from what you have seen at home. Some will be positive, and some won't. We are human. We are not perfect.

The knowledge about yourself, about why you act the way you do and how those decisions come from your parents and ancestors, is by far one of the most powerful tools I have learned in my spiritual path. Recently, about three months ago, I attended my first Family Constellations. Many friends of mine had done it in the past and had often encouraged me to do so. But I felt I had to do it when the time was right, following divine timing. I went to work on my issues with my mother. As I already mentioned to you, I haven't had a relationship with her since I was about 14 years old.

Not only did I learn aspects about my mother that I never considered, but also (and more importantly) I learned about all of those aspects of my mother that live *in me*, as I have a 50% of biological material from her. At the same time, 50% of my mother's biological material is from my grandmother and 50% is from my grandfather, people I have never met.

See how important it is, the knowledge of the ones before you? They live inside of you my friend. It's biology. Traumas remain in your genetic material and may create traumas for you today, in this physical lifetime, and you unconsciously make choices based on those traumas you're not even aware of. Now, I know what you are saying. "Farah, how can a therapist in the Family Constellations tell you all this information if they are a stranger?" I do not have an answer for this. What comes to my mind is magic. Just like faith and gravity, it exists even though we can't see it. So my answer is to try it. You will see for yourself how incredible it is.

But there are some points that I want you to be aware before you plan to do Family Constellations:

1. Make sure you are prepared and that the time is right. Participating in Family Constellations opens a lot of floodgates in you or, as I like to call them, windows of awakening. It is often recommended that you have an understanding of yourself from previous therapy: coaching, counseling, psychotherapy, or whatever started the path to understanding your identity. If you have some knowledge of who you are, all the information that will come to you will work on a deeper level and in a more useful way. Otherwise, most of the insights you will get about you and your family won't resonate with you.

2. Find the best therapist possible. Do your research. Do not just go to the first one you find. You need to put yourself in good hands! There are amazing ones all around the world with years of experience. Ask for feedback about them. As these therapies are becoming more popular, there are lots of people who call themselves "systemic therapists" but who have no clue what they are doing. Just like every other kind of therapy, always put yourself in the best hands possible!

3. Be open-minded. Embrace the unknown, and do not question it or try to force logic on what you are not ready to fully understand. Humanity is still evolving, and many things we thought were not possible 50 years ago are so obvious to us today. The same holds true for these therapies. They are still not that mainstream, but who knows if in 50 years from now they will be part of daily care, like going to the gym?

What can your life look like after you do this Family Constellation therapy? You are resetting your subconscious mind, literally changing your energy. Once you change your subconscious, you will start to make decisions differently, to act differently. I cannot tell you what your life will look like, but I can tell you about something incredibly strange and unexplainable that happened to me. The first day after my Family Constellation therapy, I literally started eating healthy foods that I had never eaten before! My brain simply chose the healthier food without any conscious thought or willpower. Before, I had been filling my stomach but not nurturing myself with the right food. Suddenly, I started automatically choosing the healthier food.

Notice that these spiritual tips have nothing to do with religion. It's all spirituality. Humanity is spiritual. We are all spiritual energy, and we all come from nature, the power of the cells, genetics, and our environment.

Chapter 27

BE READY TO RE-CENTER

The possibility of falling off the track is always going to be around the corner, my friend. You may have come far in your fashion career. You may have enough experience to deal with all the deadlines and egos in the industry. And, yet, you may find yourself at the limit. The fashion industry can be so overwhelming, and so can life itself. It's frustrating sometimes to see that you have to work so hard to achieve balance and that you may lose it in a second if you are not alert. There are many factors that may contribute to feeling suddenly at the end of your rope, often from your sense of responsibility as a freelancer and giving priority to the client and the project instead of yourself. And this is wrong. As long as we are in this human body, this will be the game, centered or off-centered, no matter how many years you've studied the Kabbalah or Buddhism or Yoga or anything else.

We are all in this together. I struggle from time to time, just as you do and will continue to do. What I most want you to remember is that the fashion industry is full of humans. Every fashion company, small or large, mass market or luxury, is made by people. So be prepared and conscious about how you are interacting with the people around you. It is a constant and daily process to recognize that choices coming from fear and not from the heart may get you off track. I have learned recently that it is crucial to make yearly, monthly, weekly, even daily reviews of how things are going, how I am committing to my values and all the promises I made to myself when I made the shift from employee to freelancer. So, ask yourself: am I sticking to the promises I made to myself back then, or am I compromising them because of the everyday issues and clients' requests? Remember to always be honest with yourself. As Diane von Furstenberg says, the best relationship you will have in life is the relationship you have with you.

There is another reason why you will experience the need to reevaluate everything and re-center yourself: growth. After years of freelancing and consulting, you will feel the need to go to the next level. This may come as the opportunity to partner with someone or build a business. In any case, it is a new chapter with new challenges, and you need to train your mind for it. For example, in my case, I am in the process of transitioning from services to products. This book is part of that process, too. I realized that it was time for me to help as many people as possible in this industry, and how I can do this? By putting all the knowledge and experiences I have collected over the years into products that have a reduced cost and that everyone can buy. My services as a consultant have high fees, based on almost 15 years of experience, and I want to advise and mentor all the people who may need my support, not just the ones who can afford it.

But making these types of changes is not easy. You need to stretch yourself and learn things that are new for you. For example, writing a book. And believe me, it is very scary and overwhelming, but if you stick to your heart's desire, listen to your inner-voice, and know 100% that the Universe has your back, everything is going to be fine. As long as you do things from the heart with the true intention to help others and contribute to improving things, everything will be fine. I promise you.

Putting Yourself Out There and Fighting With Fear

We live in a digital era, and the next generations will live their lives on screen. When times evolve, we need to evolve with them. It is the greatest thing about humanity. In the same way fashion companies are embracing social media and other new technologies to communicate with the new generation of customers, you as a freelancer need to do so as well. I teach and sell products that I have created for personal branding among other content. I have created workbooks and e-learning courses based on the high demand from clients and students to support them with this, because the industry is requesting this. Especially if you work for creative industries, it is mandatory that you have your personal brand built into everything you sell.

Building your personal branding profile, nowadays, involves putting yourself out there so that you are visible. You'll need to have a presence on all of the different digital platforms that exist for fashion users: Facebook, Instagram, LinkedIn, Pinterest, YouTube, and who knows what platform will be next around the corner. As you start to become more visible, the battle with yourself will be huge, especially if you are a private person. I have battled with my own visibility recently.

I know videos are now a huge way to communicate in a faster and more direct way with my customers, but—oh my dear—this means I have to film myself! The first few times I filmed myself was a nightmare. I hated my voice. I hated the fact that I didn't know how to use a camera, so I had to use the camera on my phone. But little by little, I am figuring out how to be myself in this new world of video.

If you are a freelancer building your profile and want customers to find you, using some of these social media channels may be the next move you need to make in order to find long-term success. You do not have to go crazy and use all the social media in the world, but you can choose the platform that resonates more with you and with your potential customers and invest your time and energy in that one platform.

Being prepared to step out of your comfort zone is a key soft skill you need to embrace as a freelancer. There are many resources you can turn to as you step up in visibility.

- Read motivational books from the best self-development and spiritual gurus out there.

- Hire a coach. It is a great resource to have someone mentoring you to help you grow and putting yourself out there to be visible in the world.

- Ask for feedback from your clients and customers. You will be surprised to find that they can't wait for you to write that book, create that product, or film that documentary.

Often others see our gifts and talents more clearly than we do. And, yet, I am asking you to step up and to be visible, because I believe that you and I have great, revolutionary work to do, especially in this fashion world that we love so much. I believe you and I are called to be light workers of the fashion industry. Sound interesting? Turn the page, and join me.

Chapter 28

WE ARE LIGHT WORKERS OF THE FASHION INDUSTRY

Now, it's time for you to contribute to the fashion industry in a positive way. If you still have love and passion for this industry after all the struggles, you have been called to help improve things. I like to picture us as light workers in the fashion industry. Many people say that we are in the era of information and consciousness, that all around us there are millions of people who are making amazing changes, positive ones in other industries.

Fashion cannot live forever in a bubble. We are not a cliché, snobbish, self-involved island. Fashion is a creative industry, touching society at every level every day. We dress the world. We have a huge impact on the environment because of how we produce things and how we dictate social trends. And I believe we *have* to take responsibility for all this. If the world is changing, we need to evolve with it.

I think the time for healing and improvement has arrived for the fashion industry. In tiny bits, we are seeing people making positive changes. From small brands to big ones, even institutions, people are embracing a new direction that goes beyond revenues and incorporates the human aspect. I hope, in a very humble way, that this book starts a movement, even if it's just a small one—*something*. I hope that if these words resonate with you, we can create together a group of "light workers" in the fashion industry.

As light workers, our mission is to always prioritize the human in every decision we make. We make decisions from love and not fear. We apply spiritual and self-development techniques in our daily routines and methodology to improve things around us. We focus and listen to our inner voice, our intuition, and our soul, and we follow their wisdom. We will be like the good bacteria living inside our bodies, and we will start healing the organism of the fashion industry from the inside by spreading love and light. We will clean the industry from the inside out, as we grow and clean ourselves. I hope we will become hundreds, maybe even *thousands* of light workers in the fashion industry. We will start small, but we will be powerful. Small groups of people have made the difference in the world. History is full of them. As a group, we have the power to commit to do what is right, not what is ego driven.

We can start with our own choices, and this will be particular to our own, individual values. If what most resonates with you is the huge environmental impact that fashion industry has in a negative way, then start with your own shopping behavior. Buy fewer and better quality goods. Gather information about where and how the brands you buy are produced and how they treat workers. When a friend compliments something you have bought, tell her *why* you bought it. It is obvious, I know, but the fact is that by and large, we do not do it. If you have the courage to do it, others will do it, too.

Your values will make a difference in the type of clients and projects you accept. Go back to the heart-driven companies vs. fear-driven companies, and pick your side well. Do not give your time, wisdom, and energy to someone or something you do not believe in. Their priorities will drown your values, and you will add to the problem rather than become a solution.

We have the amazing gift of feeling deep in our guts what is the right thing to do. God, the Universe, or Mother Nature gave this intuition to us, among thousands of other gifts. But we also have our ego, which presents obstacles to making the right decision in every way. Pay attention, take your time, improve your life by embracing a spiritual lifestyle, and you will be more driven to be at peace and make the right choices.

Let's do it, fashion light worker! Let's make changes together, and let's start the healing process in this industry. We are not alone, not anymore, because others are starting the movement with different names, versions, and techniques, but in the end the goal is the same: to heal, change, improve, and move humanity into the next chapter of evolution.

As Seth Godin says, let's create a tribe! And I propose a movement of fashion light workers. If you want to know more about me and the tribe of ambitious, spiritual, centered, fashion light workers, please join us here:

www.farahlizpallaro.com

I can't wait to see you on the other side.

Acknowledgments

This is by far the most difficult part of writing this book. I have so many people I would like to thank that I am terrified that I may forget someone!

This is my first book—yes, now I know I will write others, remember the inner voice? She is still talking to me louder and louder ;)—so I want to thank the ones who contributed, many times without knowing it, to writing this book as they contributed to my life journey.

My students, all of them, the present, the future, and the past ones. I cannot express with words how much I owe you. During my eight years of teaching, I've received messages of gratitude from you because of what you have learned about the fashion industry, as well as your words and life! But what you do not know is how much you have contributed to helping me understand, discover, and embrace one of my biggest passions: to teach and to mentor. I never thought this was going to be one of the most life-changing paths for me. An important part of this book is for you.

My peers and colleagues of the fashion industry, to the ones I had good relationships with and to the ones I had bad relationships, as well. You all have helped me to build a deep understanding of the dynamics, systems, and expertise of this industry, and without this, I couldn't write this book.

My friends, I often say that friends are the family you choose! I do not have to give names, you know who you are. Thank you for the encouragement, the support, and believing in me more than I do! Thank you for all those moments where I felt unworthy and you helped me to the other side. Thank you, from all my heart!

My family, all of you, my amazing brother and beautiful sisters, my nephews, cousins, aunts, uncles, sister-in-law, and stepmother for always challenging me. Yes, I am Italian, we have huge families! ;) I thank you for both the good moments as well as the bad ones. Some of you have been by far the most difficult people I've had to deal with but also the people I love the most. Some of you have been a mirror of constant learning for me.

My father, thank you for that 50% of you that lives in me and for teaching me about business, discipline, and grounding. I have learned that even if we may look two worlds apart we have more things in common than what we both realize.

My mother, thank you for bringing me to this world and giving me the opportunity to live my life path. You could have made a different decision 40 years ago. Now I know you were already lost back then, but you chose to give me the best gift possible, the gift of life. I feel grateful and blessed to have found you again and to have had the opportunity, even if from distance, to learn about you within me. I learned that my passion for beauty, creativity, spirituality, and intuition comes from you. And I am embracing you every day and all our females ancestors who are constantly teaching me how to lead.

And, finally, I wish to thank the most important person in my life, my inner child. The people who know me best know that I have this bad habit of always putting others before me. Well, I have learned also during the journey of writing this book the importance of nurturing my inner self, my inner child. While I was teaching you this in the book, I was teaching this to myself, as well. So, I want to thank that inner child who lives in me, the one who believes that everything is possible, the one who makes me see the world through a beautiful and positive lens, the one who always looks to give unconditional love to the world by being in service to others... I love you, and I value you, and I would never ever abandon you.

References

General:
Deepak Chopra: www.deepakchopra.com
Wayne Dyer: www.drwaynedyer.com
Susan Ferraro: www.susanf.com
Louise Hay: www.louisehay.com
Esther and Jerry Hicks: www.abraham-hicks.com/
lawofattractionsource/index.php
Jennifer McLean: www.mcleanmasterworks.com
Eckhart Tolle: www.eckharttolle.com
Brad Yates: www.tapwithbrad.com

Page 26
Your Erroneous Zones by Wayne Dyer
Creative Visualization by Shakti Gawain
The Power is Within You by Louise Hay
Ask And It Is Given by Esther and Jerry Hicks
The Power of Now by Eckhart Tolle
Live in the Moment by Eckhart Tolle

Page 45
The Creative Pathfinder by Mark McGuiness
The Element by Ken Robison
The Little Prince by Antoine de Saint-Exupéry

Page 48
The Concise Dictionary of Dress by Judith Clark and Adam Phillips
Dries Van Noten by Pamela Golbin
Papercraft: Design and Art with Paper by Robert Klanten and Sven Ehmann
Content Triumph of Realization by Rem Koolhaas and Brendan McGetrick
Inkspired by Betty Soldi

Page 50
Chakra Balancing: Body, Mind & Soul by Deepak Chopra

Page 80
The Law of Attraction: The Basics of the Teachings of Abraham by Esther and Jerry Hicks